WRITING FOR
Success

Preparing for

BUSINESS, TECHNOLOGY,

TRADES, and CAREER PROGRAMS

DALE FITZPATRICK

KATHLEEN CENTER VANCE

British Columbia Institute of Technology

Prentice Hall Allyn and Bacon Canada
Don Mills, Ontario

Canadian Cataloguing in Publication Data

Fitzpatrick, Dale Mary, 1959-
Writing for Success: preparing for business, technology, trades and career programs

ISBN 978-0-13-095493-0

1. Technical writing.   2. Business writing. 3. English language - Technical English. 4.
English language - Business English. 5. English language - Textbooks for second
language learners.* I. Vance, Kathleen Center. II. Title.

T11.F57 1998   808'.0666   C97-932815-2

Prentice-Hall, Inc., Upper Saddle River, New Jersey
Prentice-Hall International (UK) Limited, London
Prentice-Hall of Australia, Pty. Limited, Sydney
Prentice-Hall Hispanoamericana, S.A., Mexico City
Prentice-Hall of India Private Limited, New Delhi
Prentice-Hall of Japan, Inc., Tokyo
Simon & Schuster Asia Private Limited, Singapore
Editora Prentice-Hall do Brasil, Ltda., Rio de Janeiro

ISBN 978-0-13-095493-0

Vice President, Editorial Director: Laura Pearson
Executive Developmental Editor: Marta Tomins
Marketing Manager: Jodie Blaney
Production Editor: Susan James
Copy Editor: Sharon Kirsch
Production Coordinator: Wendy Moran
Permissions/Photo Research: Susan Wallace-Cox
Cover Design: Julia Hall
Cover Image: Photonica/Masaaki Kazama
Page Layout: Dave McKay

4 5 6 7 8 9 A G M V 0 9 8

TABLE OF CONTENTS

CHAPTER 1: IDENTIFYING YOUR READER AND PURPOSE BEFORE YOU WRITE

CHAPTER 2: PUTTING YOUR MAIN IDEA FIRST IN EVERY SENTENCE

CHAPTER 3: COMBINING YOUR SENTENCES TO SHOW THE RELATIONSHIP BETWEEN YOUR IDEAS

CHAPTER 4: WRITING IN A TECHNICAL STYLE: CHOOSING YOUR WORDS CAREFULLY

CHAPTER 5: ORGANIZING YOUR IDEAS INTO PARAGRAPHS

CHAPTER 6: USING HEADINGS AND LISTS TO HELP YOUR READER

APPENDIX: GUIDELINES 189

INTRODUCTION FOR TEACHERS

We are practising teachers with many years' experience teaching English as a second language, and teaching technical and business writing courses to post-secondary students in engineering and health technologies, business, and trades. In community and college programs, we have taught ESL students at all levels, from beginner to intermediate to advanced. During the fifteen years we have spent working with business, technology, and trades programs, we have interviewed employers, former students, and technology instructors to find out exactly what skills students in those programs need to succeed in their studies and in their future careers. In *Writing for Success*, we offer you and your students the experience and wisdom we have gained from teaching in both of these challenging fields: ESL, and business and technical communication.

WRITING FOR SUCCESS IS FOR STUDENTS DESTINED FOR BUSINESS AND TECHNICAL WORKPLACES.

The purpose of this textbook is to prepare non-native and native speakers for first-year post-secondary studies in business, vocational, and technology programs. This textbook can also be used with ESL students already enrolled in first-year programs who need language support, for example, students in English for business programs. *Writing for Success* can also be used as a supplementary textbook for students in first-year business communication or technical writing courses. The textbook, because of its many work-related examples and exercises, can also be used with students already employed in business and technical workplaces.

Writing for Success teaches the formats and styles of workplace writing. Because it provides teachers with many real-world exercises for students to apply their grammar skills, *Writing for Success* is an excellent complement to any grammar textbook you may be using with your students.

This textbook can be used with students interested in program areas as diverse as accounting, nursing, welding, and computer systems. *Writing for Success* uses examples and exercises that draw on content from many fields, and the formats and styles taught are common to all of them. Unlike textbooks, for example, which specialize in the vocabulary and communication tasks for one particular field, our text teaches the language and communication skills students need to write in all of their fields of study.

WRITING FOR SUCCESS FEATURES AN ABUNDANCE OF EXERCISES TO TEACH STUDENTS THE BASICS OF TECHNICAL AND BUSINESS WRITING STYLES.

Writing for Success covers the basic principles of technical writing style and includes plenty of exercises, examples, and illustrations that are relevant, practical, and designed to appeal to students. The examples, models, and exercises of this content-based textbook are drawn from practical, technical, and business writing. Students learn how to write standard business letters and memos for such practical purposes as telling their supervisors when they're available for work, disputing bills, and reporting office break-ins. Unlike a composition textbook that might require students to write an essay on the importance of creating the "green" workplace or the role played by computers in the workplace, *Writing for Success* requires students to write a memo recommending switching to energy-saving fluorescent lighting for a seventeen-unit apartment building, or to revise a memo recommending precautions for employees to protect company files from computer viruses.

WRITING FOR SUCCESS **SUPPORTS A VARIETY OF TEACHING STRATEGIES AND EASILY FITS DIVERSE POPULATIONS OF STUDENTS.**

Learning outcomes are explicitly stated for each chapter and supported by a variety of teaching strategies, including the use of tables and other key visuals, pair work and group work, pre-writing strategies, and activities that integrate speaking, listening, writing, and critical-thinking skills.

Writing for Success can be effectively used with non-native and native speakers, in separate classes or integrated into one class. Expository text is minimal. Students are not faced with long pages of text telling them how to write, and the fundamentals of business and technical writing are explained at a language level all students can understand. Cultural and linguistic background materials are provided for the exercises, so that ESL students can participate fully. *Writing for Success* is written to include all students: male and female; of all "looks" and sizes, ages, and ethnic origins; from across Canada and from around the world.

The textbook is designed for today's goal-oriented students. Each chapter contains writing exercises that, when the students have completed them successfully, constitute finished products that students can incorporate into their portfolios and present to future employers as samples of their business and technical writing skills.

WRITING FOR SUCCESS **ADDRESSES THE STUDENTS' MOST IMPORTANT WRITING NEEDS BY FOCUSING ON THE WORD, SENTENCE, AND PARA-GRAPH LEVELS.**

Writing for Success is both a language and a communication textbook. Each chapter opens with outcomes in both areas, so the students can see how the areas are interrelated. In contrast with first-year business and technical writing textbooks, *Writing for Success* focuses on the students' language at levels where they most need help: at the word, sentence, and paragraph levels. This focus also allows students to appreciate the similarities between business and technical writing and the writing they have been doing for their academic or general interest classes, and thus to build on the skills they have already developed. Students will also experience the important, far-reaching differences between business and technical writing and academic and general interest writing, and thus appreciate the need for this separate textbook on the formats and styles of workplace writing.

WRITING FOR SUCCESS **IS ORGANIZED SO STUDENTS KNOW WHAT THEY ARE LEARNING AND WHY, AND HAVE AMPLE OPPORTUNITIES TO DEMON-STRATE THEIR LEARNING.**

Each of the six chapters of *Writing for Success* includes the following:

- An **Introduction** that explains the importance of the concepts and skills taught in the context of business and technical writing.

- Communication and language **Learning Outcomes** that help students keep track of their specific learning.

- **Guidelines** preceded and followed by explanations. Guidelines are general directions for how to write. Students need to practise critical thinking and sound judgment to know when and how to apply the guidelines. An example would be a guideline for organizing information in letters and memos. Students are also given rules, but these, unlike guidelines, are meant to be applied "to the letter," without discretion. An example would be a punctuation rule or a rule for forming the passive voice.

- **Tables** that summarize important information the students will want to consult often when they write. An example would be a table of coordinating conjunctions and their meanings.

- **Practices**, interspersed throughout the chapter, which allow students to check their understanding of the concepts and their ability to apply them before they move on to the next concept.

- **Review Questions** that allow students to ensure they have learned the most important concepts of the chapter.

- A **Question Sheet** for students to record any unanswered questions at the end of each chapter. Students are encouraged to find the answers from other students or their teacher and record them in their textbook.

- **Exercises** that allow students to apply their skills at the sentence, paragraph, and whole-document levels. Students are given the overall contexts for all exercises, including those at the sentence level. Several exercises are included for each chapter, so the teacher and the students can choose those that will interest and help them most.

Chapter 1 introduces students to the two basic concepts of business and technical writing: audience and purpose. Chapter 1 also introduces students to the formats of letters, memos, and informal and formal reports. Because Chapter 1 presents the basic concepts and formats, it is the longest chapter in the book. Chapters 2 and 3 focus on sentences, while Chapter 4 focuses on words. In Chapter 5, students learn to apply what they've learned about words and sentences by writing effective paragraphs. Chapter 5 contains the most exercises of all the chapters in order to give students plenty of practice consolidating what they've learned in the first five chapters. Finally, Chapter 6 teaches students how to use headings and lists to highlight information.

Technology is the study of the practical, of what works, and the critical part of *Writing for Success* lies in the exercises, where the students apply the guidelines to writing for the real world.

INTRODUCTION FOR STUDENTS

We have written this book to teach you the writing skills you need to be well prepared to succeed in business, technology, trades, and career programs.

The job of your teachers is to help you, so if you have any questions about any part of this book, ask your teacher. Your job is to read the book, complete the exercises, and ask for whatever help you need in the most important task you will undertake in your career: learning how to write successfully.

We have taught many students to write more successfully. Our students have been preparing to enter business, technology, trades, and career programs; or they have already been enrolled in their programs; or they have already been working in their fields. We have always measured our success in teaching students to write by *their* success in their studies and in the workplace; for example, if you are preparing to study financial management, it is your accounting teacher, and finally your supervisor in the workplace and your clients, who will judge if you are a successful writer. Your writing teachers are here to help you learn how to write, but your future employers, clients, and customers will have the last word.

We have found that you don't need any special talents to write successfully. You'll need the same skills you'll be using to succeed in your career whether, for example, as a computer analyst, electronics technician, interior designer, or occupational health and safety inspector. You will need to identify the work that needs to be done, in this case, the writing task. You will need to apply the guidelines, which we will teach you, to the specific writing task and to pay attention to every detail. You will need to anticipate and take care of any problems and to double-check that the job has been completed correctly. And, just as in your career, you'll have to complete the work by the deadline, as efficiently as you can.

As you progress through each chapter of this book, you will learn guidelines that will show you how to complete your school and workplace writing tasks correctly and efficiently. We will show you how to write the kinds of documents you'll need to write in your career. You'll learn to write in the friendly, direct style favoured by Canadian business. You will be able to practise your writing as you complete exercises that are based on the writing tasks you can expect to be doing in the workplace.

At the beginning of each chapter we will tell you the learning outcomes, so you will know what you are expected to learn in that chapter. We will also tell you why you need to learn the material. We will give you many examples to help you understand the guidelines presented. The review questions will help you check that you understand the guidelines, and the exercises will tell you how well you know how to apply the guidelines in your writing.

Enjoy this book, and approach your writing tasks as you would all the other jobs you will be learning to do in your career: with commitment, confidence, and enthusiasm.

ACKNOWLEDGMENTS

We thank David Kipling, British Columbia Institute of Technology instructor, who teaches technical writing to students in fish and wildlife, forestry, and geographical information systems, and who read every word of this book. We found his suggested editorial changes extremely helpful, although any flaws in the book are our own. Unlike many people, David is endlessly excited by the work of editing, and like a race car mechanic, he is always looking for the tiny improvement that will make a winning sentence. Thank you, David, for all your contributions.

We also thank Jonathan Candy, British Columbia Institute of Technology instructor in geographical information systems, for providing technical background for some of the exercises in this book. Again, any inaccuracies are our own.

For taking time to read all or part of the manuscript, and for their varied and valuable suggestions, we thank Sarah Bowers of the University of British Columbia, Louis Buchanan of Ryerson Polytechnic University, Pamela Idahosa of George Brown College, Marlene Allard-Lutynski of the British Columbia Institute of Technology, and Virginia Reid of Sheridan College.

ABOUT THE AUTHORS

DALE FITZPATRICK

Dale Fitzpatrick has an MA in Language Education from the University of British Columbia. A Newfoundlander, she completed a B Jour at Carleton University in Ottawa and worked as a journalist for the *Evening Telegram* in St. John's, Newfoundland. She then worked as publications officer for the Department of Forestry and for the Department of Mines and Energy in Newfoundland. After teaching journalism for three years, Dale moved to British Columbia and continued teaching at Douglas College, Kwantlen University College, Vancouver Community College, English Language Institute at the University of British Columbia, and now at the British Columbia Institute of Technology (BCIT).

At BCIT she has taught students in forestry, financial management, marketing, nuclear medicine, and occupational health and safety. She also enjoys teaching students preparing to enter programs at BCIT and has served as program head of BCIT's Pre-Entry Program for seven years.

Dale and Kathleen have worked on many projects together. Most recently they developed modules using computer-mediated communication to teach language and employability skills, and modules for intermediate-level English language training students for the British Columbia Ministry of Education, Skills and Training.

KATHLEEN VANCE

Kathleen Vance has a PhD in Germanic Languages and Literature from the University of British Columbia. Born in New York, she earned a BA in Philosophy, Phi Beta Kappa, from the State University of New York. While completing her MA in German from California State University, she also worked as a ghostwriter. She has worked as a consultant for an international engineering firm in Vancouver, and has also taught a special program to technology instructors at Ming Chuan College in Taipei. In Prince Rupert, British Columbia, Kathleen taught a special program to students working in the electrical and mechanical trades.

Graduates who have completed Kathleen's communication courses at BCIT work in pulp and paper mills, sawmills, electronics firms, research laboratories, industrial plants, acute care hospitals, resort hotels, and in many other industries in Canada, the United States, Libya, Lebanon, Thailand, and throughout the world.

chapter one

IDENTIFYING YOUR READER AND PURPOSE BEFORE YOU WRITE

Our students are always telling us how much work they are expected to do and how little time they have to do it. Later, when our graduates come back to see us, they tell us how busy their workplaces are. Writing will be a major part of your work at school and on the job. If you follow the guidelines in this chapter, you will learn to plan and finish your writing tasks more efficiently.

You will learn how to identify your readers and your purpose before you write, so that you will be able to plan what information to include. You will find that filling out a plan sheet will save time for you and your busy readers.

Communication Outcomes

When you finish this chapter, you will be able to

- identify the purpose of writing according to what your reader needs and wants to know
- make an outline before you start to write to make sure your purpose stands out clearly and you include all the details in the right order
- put your main idea (purpose) first in your writing
- group details that are related
- arrange details in the order in which your reader expects and needs to see them
- end by stating the precise action you want your reader to actually perform
- use a standard Canadian format for your letters and memos
- explain the purpose of the subject line in a memo or letter
- revise your writing to correct for prejudices that would offend some readers
- talk to others to clarify your purpose before you write
- use a checklist to evaluate and revise your writing after you've written.

Language Outcomes

When you finish this chapter, you will be able to

- write a purpose statement
- write a main idea sentence based on a purpose statement
- revise business letters and memos by adding missing main idea sentences, reordering sentences, and deleting sentences that are not related to main ideas
- write subject lines that are specific and concise
- use nouns and pronouns that include both women and men when appropriate
- revise your writing to correct any errors in pronoun agreement.

DEFINING YOUR PURPOSE

Look at the following example of a letter to VISA in which the writer did not identify clearly her reader and purpose before she started writing. In the following pages, you will learn how the writer could have written a more successful letter more efficiently.

LETTER TO VISA

1050 Breeze Hill
Ottawa, ON K1P 1J3

August 16, 199—

Domestic Customer Services
P.O. Box 4100
Postal Station "A"
Toronto, ON M5W 1T1

Dear Sir

When I'm not working at my job as a software engineer, I like to race my motor-cycle, a YSR 80 cc. I'm a member of the Nifty 50 Club, and every summer for the past few years, I have travelled from Ottawa to Hamilton to race in the annual Nifty 50 Club 50cc Series.

On June 20, about a month before the race, I phoned the Snooze Inn in Hamilton to reserve a room for Tuesday, July 22, and Wednesday, July 23, because I knew I wouldn't get to Hamilton until around 9 p.m. on July 22 and wanted to make sure I would have somewhere to stay when I arrived. When I told the reservations clerk over the phone that I would not be arriving until after 6 p.m., she asked me for my credit card number in order to keep my reservation until 9 p.m. That's when I gave my VISA number.

When I arrived in Hamilton on Tuesday, July 22, the weekend of the race, I checked in at the Snooze Inn. Unfortunately, the hotel's computer reservation system wasn't working when I got there. I managed to get a room, but the desk clerk on duty said that, because the computer was down, he had no record to show that I had already charged the room to my VISA. I explained that I'd understood the room had already been charged to my VISA when I'd booked over the phone. He charged the room to my VISA again and assured me that, if the reservation records showed the room had already been charged to my VISA when I'd booked on June 20, the second charge to my VISA would be torn up.

However, when I received my August statement from VISA this week, I discovered that the Snooze Inn had billed me twice for my room reservation. My bill shows two charges for $160 each, both from the Snooze Inn and both for the same dates. I should have been charged only once.

It looks like there was some mix up at the hotel. The desk clerk who originally took my reservation over the phone did charge the room to my VISA, and I was charged again when I arrived at the hotel on July 22.

I called the hotel to explain the mistake, but they told me I would have to get the mistake corrected through the VISA office. It should be obvious that I'm telling the truth here, since it would not be possible for me to stay in two rooms at the same time, at the same hotel, and on the same two days. So, I phoned the VISA office in Toronto earlier today and explained the situation to a VISA representative. He told me I would have to write a letter detailing the problem.

For the reasons listed above, I would like the mistake on my VISA bill to be corrected as soon as possible. By the way, I've already paid my August bill because I always pay all my bills when they're due no matter what.

Sincerely

Francine Beaulieu

Francine Beaulieu

What is your opinion of the letter to VISA? Is it successful? Do you think it was difficult to write? Do you think it is difficult for a VISA representative to understand? In the next few pages we'll rewrite the letter to show you how you can make your letters more successful and easier to write.

Key Term

PURPOSE: *The reason you are writing and the results you expect from your writing.*

All effective writing starts from a clearly defined **purpose**. But many people begin to write before they have figured out *why* they are writing, before they have asked themselves what results they expect to get from their writing. Because they haven't *defined their purpose*, their writing lacks focus; it tries to say too much, wanders away from the point, or misses the point altogether!

It's a good idea to state your purpose at the beginning of a letter or memo, if possible. That way, your readers can see right away what it is you want them to do.

GUIDELINE 1:

State your purpose at the beginning of your letters and memos.

Remember: If you don't know your purpose in writing, your readers won't know it either.

To define your purpose, you must answer a basic question, "What do I want to happen as a result of writing this?"

In this case, the answer might be, "I want VISA to give me a credit for the $160 overcharge."

As we said, you should state your purpose at the very beginning of a letter or memo. That means you need a good opening sentence, and to write that sentence, you must answer to yourself another basic question: "What simple statement will express this purpose to my reader?"

In this case, the answer might be: "I would like a credit for the overcharge."

Now you may think this looks very blunt. Don't worry; we can alter the wording and the position later. Right now we have taken a very important step: **clearly stating our purpose.**

GUIDELINE 2:

Phrase your purpose statement by answering the question "What do I want my reader to do?"

Phrasing a purpose statement clearly like this helps you to write. Now you'll be able to narrow your topic, stick to the point, avoid unnecessary details later on, and organize your message properly.

DEFINING YOUR READER

Key Terms

READERS AND READER NEEDS: *The people you are writing to and the information they need in order to do what you want them to do.*

Just as people forget to define their purpose, they also often **forget to take into account the people who will be reading their writing**. Defining your readers is important because who you are writing to will affect what you say and the way you say it.

Define your readers after you've defined your purpose. Answer the question, "Who are my readers going to be?" Try to picture your readers, and estimate how much they already know about your subject.

Picturing Your Reader

As you imagine your readers, try to correct for any prejudices you may have that would prevent you from seeing *all* your probable readers. You may have prejudices based on gender, physical or mental disability, a person's origins, or a person's looks.

Take, for example, the case of the letter to the customer service representative at VISA. If you can only imagine a service representative who is a man, you may begin your letter with "Dear Sir." But suppose the customer service representative were a woman. She might find "Dear Sir" so offensive, she wouldn't want to grant your request for a credit. Try to write without prejudice, so you won't offend any of your readers.

Practice

Pretend you have graduated from a business, technology, trades, or career program and are working in industry. You are writing to the other business people, technicians, and technologists you work with. Close your eyes and picture your readers.

Now open your eyes and look around your classroom. (If you are trying this at home, you'll have to wait until your next class or remember your classmates and picture them around you.) Do the readers you pictured look like the students sitting in your classroom? If your picture doesn't match that of the students in your room, **correct your picture** of your readers. Remember, the students sitting around you are your future co-workers.

GUIDELINE 3:

Include *all* your probable readers when you write.

Do not use words like "Sir," which refer only to men, when your reader may be a woman. Similarly, do not use gender pronouns when your reader may be either a woman or a man. Gender pronouns are pronouns that refer only to men (he, his, him) or only to women (she, her).

Using language that includes *all* readers is extremely important when writing in the workplace. It's not fair to leave people out; it's bad business, and, in some cases, may even violate human rights law. Treating people unfairly by excluding them also causes employers to lose the goodwill of many of their employees, customers, and clients.

Anticipating Your Reader's Questions

Once you've accurately pictured your reader, **figure out probable questions your reader will ask, and answer those questions in your writing.** Taking into account your reader's probable questions will help you determine what to say, in what order to say it, and how much or how little you need to say.

Thus, you should try to think of yourself not only as the writer but as the reader of your writing. If you do this, you will find it easier to write clearly and understandably.

Now that you've learned how to define your purpose and your reader, and to anticipate your reader's questions, you should be able to fill in a plan sheet similar to the following rough plan sheet for the VISA letter. However, the rough plan sheet does not tell you the order in which to present the information to your reader. For that, you will need to make an outline.

ROUGH PLAN SHEET FOR THE LETTER TO VISA

Who is my reader?	a customer service representative in the Domestic Services Office for VISA
What will my reader need to know *first*?	that I want her or him to give me credit for an over-charge
What other things will my reader need to be told?	that I was charged twice on my August bill for the same room on the same dates, the name of the hotel I stayed at, and the dates and the room rate I was charged
	that I charged the room for two nights over the phone
	that the hotel reservations system computer was down and I had to charge the room to my VISA again
	my explanation for the overcharge
	what to do next (credit the overcharge to my next month's bill)

The rough plan sheet above sums up what's needed in our letter to VISA. Now take a moment to look at the first letter again to see how lack of planning encouraged the writer to ramble aimlessly and to include unnecessary information.

Items the customer service representative didn't need to be told include the following:

- your job
- your reason for travelling to Hamilton
- your conversation with VISA
- what the hotel desk clerk said
- that you don't think it's possible to stay in two rooms at the same time
- that you race YSR 50 cc's.

Now that we have a rough plan sheet, we know

- WHY we're writing
- WHO we're writing to
- WHAT our reader needs to know.

All that's left is to put it in order.

MAKING YOUR OUTLINE

Key Term

OUTLINE: *The order in which you present your main ideas.*

Key Term

MAIN IDEA: *A major idea that is the basis for a paragraph.*

Key Term

MAIN IDEA SENTENCE: *The sentence that introduces a paragraph.*

You know your purpose. You know your reader. You know what you need to say to the reader.

Now you must rough out an **outline**. To make an outline, you must decide what order to put your main ideas in.

You've already learned to put your purpose first, so your first main idea will be your purpose. You've anticipated your reader's questions, so you know what you need to say. Now put those main ideas in the order your reader will want to hear them.

Think of an outline as being like a grocery shopping list. Just as the shopping list helps you stay within your budget and remember everything you need, so an outline will make sure you stick to your purpose and include all the information your reader needs. Thus, just as wise shoppers always make lists before they enter the store, so successful writers will prepare outlines before they write.

GUIDELINE 4:

Prepare an outline before you write.

Here is an outline already filled in for the VISA letter.

OUTLINE FOR THE LETTER TO VISA

First main idea and details: (Purpose) I want a credit for the overcharge.

In my August VISA bill, I was double-charged for the same hotel room for the same two nights.

Second main idea and details: I reserved a room over the phone and charged the $160 for the two nights to my VISA.

The room was at the Snooze Inn at Hamilton for two nights on July 22 and 23.

Third main idea and details: When I arrived at the hotel, the hotel's reservation system computer was down, and I was asked to sign another form charging the room to my VISA.

Fourth main idea and details:	My explanation of the overcharge: The overcharge occurred as a result of my being required to charge the same room a second time after I had already charged it over the phone.
Final main idea and details:	(Clear request for action) Credit the overcharge to the next month's bill for my account (Account Number...).

Scan your outline to see if your message is logical, to see if all the ideas and details are in the right order.

Now you can write. Your outline lists the main ideas and the details. Turn each main idea into a main idea sentence that will introduce a paragraph. The paragraph will contain the details listed for that main idea in your outline.

In later chapters you'll be learning many individual writing skills; for now, we'll assume you've written the letter.

SUGGESTED REWRITE OF THE UNPLANNED LETTER

1050 Breeze Hill
Ottawa, ON
K1P 1J3

August 16, 199—

Domestic Customer Services
P.O. Box 4100
Postal Station "A"
Toronto, ON M5W 1T1

Subject: Request for Credit to VISA Account # 1234 567 890 257

In my August VISA bill, I was double-charged for the same hotel room for the same two nights. I would like a credit for the overcharge.

I reserved a room over the phone for two nights and charged it to my VISA. Here are the details of my booking:

- Hotel: Snooze Inn, Hamilton, Ontario
- Dates: July 22 and 23
- Cost: $160 for the two nights

When I arrived at the hotel, the hotel's computer reservation system was down, and I was asked to sign another form charging the room to my VISA.

Thus, the overcharge occurred as a result of my being required to charge the same room a second time, after I had already charged it over the phone.

Please credit the $160 overcharge to my September VISA bill, account number 1234 567 890 257.

Sincerely

Francine Beaulieu

Francine Beaulieu

TABLE 1.1
Comparing the planned letter and the unplanned letter

Planned Letter	Unplanned Letter
Starts by announcing the purpose.	Reader's reaction: "Why are you telling me?" and "What does this have to do with me?"
Continues with the brief, relevant facts.	Jumps from topic to topic.
States the problem briefly and clearly.	Includes many details the reader doesn't need or want to know.
Ends with a clear request.	Ends vaguely.
Overall, is simple, clear, and polite.	Overall, is difficult to understand and annoyingly disorganized.

You've probably noticed something else: the planned letter is shorter. In fact it uses only 122 words to achieve the purpose that the other letter failed to achieve in 512 words.

A little planning saves you time in writing and saves the reader even more time in understanding.

GUIDELINE 5:

Put your main idea first and end with a precise action.

Notice on the outline for the VISA letter that the first main idea is the purpose, which is a clear statement of what you want your reader to do. The final main idea is a clear request for an action. The rewritten VISA letter, for example, begins by asking for a credit for the overcharge. The letter ends by specifying that you want the $160 credited to Account #1234 567 890 257, and that you want the credit to appear on your September bill. Thus, you will know by September if your letter has been successful because you will see the results on your bill. If you follow these two strategies, your reader will always know what you want and you, as a writer, will always know if you've been successful.

Remember:

- Put the main idea first.
- End a message with an action.

Put the Main Idea First

Think of what your reader *most needs to know*. Put this at the very beginning of your reports, letters, and memos.

Many writers are shy about using this strategy. They feel that this would "spoil the story" in the same way that peeking at the end of a novel cheats the reader of something.

Remind yourself that people who read at work *don't want stories* and *don't want suspense*. You know what they want, so be courteous and tell them in the first sentence.

Below is a letter received in reply to a complaint. Ask yourself, "What does the *reader* of this letter most need to know?", and judge how effectively the writer has ordered the information.

LETTER TO ATLANTIC MACHINE LTD.

Production Department
Atlantic Machine Ltd.

605 Terminal Avenue
Halifax, NS B3A 2M3

November 8, 199—

Ms. Maria Grzejszczak
Purchasing Engineer
Purchasing Department
Stirling-Campbell Marine Diesels
888 High Street
Halifax, NS B3A 2M3

Dear Ms. Grzejszczak

Subject: Unfinished Shafts (Shipment #PM/92/25)

In your letter of November 1 you said that the one hundred power-shafts we delivered to you on October 31 had not been finish-ground after heat treatment. This batch of components was due to be finished when a chemical spill temporarily disabled one of our machine tools. During the clean-up the unfinished shafts were inadvertently moved to our "work-completed" area and from there to our shipping department.

Thank you for alerting us to this error. We have now set up new routines that will prevent further incidents like this one.

We will deliver replacement shafts on November 6.

Sincerely

Bruce Hamersly

Bruce Hamersly
Production Engineer

The reader would like some explanation, of course, but her most immediate need is to know, "What are they doing about the shafts?"

The letter's last sentence should have been its first sentence.

In case you're curious about *finish-grinding*—*finish-grinding* of heat-treated steel is required because the heat treatment can distort workpieces above a certain size.

Next are two messages in which the main idea is placed right at the beginning, as it should be:

LETTER TO TESLA ELECTRIC

Atlantic Reforestation Ltd.

7899 Kermode Avenue
Fredericton, NB E2A 3R4

January 31, 199—

Mr. Bijan Pourkarimi
Sales Engineer
HVAC Division
Tesla Electric Canada Ltd.
7342 Broderick Road
Windsor, ON N9H 1W7

Dear Mr. Pourkarimi

Subject: Warranty Claim on Furnace Blower

I need a replacement under warranty of the gas furnace blower you installed for us last August.

The purchase was as follows:

Date: August 15, 199—
Fan: Reynard 108TNA
Invoice: 92/553
Sales Representative: Ian Twigg

The blower's bearings appeared to seize on January 30 this year, under normal operating conditions. On November 15 your local contractor checked the unit after we'd noticed a reduced air flow, but she could find nothing wrong. The fan was under no unusual stress, as our building's heating ducts had all been cleaned the week before your company installed the furnace. I have all the components ready for inspection.

Please phone me at (506) 876-2625 on February 6 to tell me when you will deliver the replacement unit. I need to hear from you by then, so I can re-schedule our production work.

Sincerely

Giuliana Miotti

Giuliana Miotti

Manager
Greenhouse Operations

MEMO TO STAFF

TO: All Staff
FROM: Kamal Chahal, Personnel Director
DATE: April 19, 199—
SUBJECT: Invitation to Orientation Meeting on Sexual
           Harassment Policy

I would like to invite all staff to attend our May 1 orientation meeting on our company's new sexual harassment policy.

Date: May 1
Time: 1300 – 1400 hrs.
Place: Staff Meeting Room (Rm. 3220)
Guest Speaker: Wayne Hwai, Regional Director, Canadian Human Rights
              Commission

Enclosed is a copy of the policy. Please come to the meeting prepared to ask questions.

K.C.

End a Message with an Action

Tell your reader the next step in the last part of your message.

Don't force the reader to go back through your writing to recheck what's to be done. Ask for or report specific action in the last sentence. Don't worry if this repeats, in detail, something you said in the first part of your letter.

Here is an action ending that is not specific enough. It may not produce action:

It would be appreciated if your company could get in touch with us at an early date to discuss this matter.

Here is an action ending that will get the job done:

Please arrange for your sales rep to call on our purchasing manager, Connie Szucs, before next Friday, November 13, with details of alternative power units and prices.

Some writers feel it is not polite to ask for specific action. They write vague, non-specific endings in the belief that this will not offend the reader.

But if such a "polite" ending involves the reader in telephoning or writing back to ask for specific times, perhaps it is not such a polite ending after all. For example, "Please contact me regarding this matter as soon as possible" could mean any of the following: please come by our office tomorrow morning, please write a reply before next Friday, please phone, or please fax your answer/your data/your decision. Be polite by being precise.

USING A STANDARD FORMAT FOR YOUR LETTERS AND MEMOS

Key Term

FORMAT: *Rules for the appearance and content of standard business and technical documents, such as letters and memos, and informal and formal reports.*

You may have noticed that of the two messages you just read, the one about the warranty claim on the furnace blower is a letter, and the one about the company's harassment policy is a memo. You may also recall that, while this chapter began with the VISA *letter*, Guideline 1 suggests you state your purpose at the beginning of your letters *and memos*. Thus, you might have wondered what exactly a memo was and what the difference was between a letter and a memo. This section of Chapter 1 will answer your questions about the formats most commonly used in writing in the workplace: letters and memos, and informal and formal reports.

Think of the last letter you received. If you left it open on your desk and looked at it from about 1 metre away, you would probably still recognize it as a letter. How would you recognize it? You'd recognize it by the way the words are arranged on the page, for example, with the addresses and the date in narrow columns, and by the main part of the letter spread from margin to margin. You would also know by the content, such as a complete handwritten signature, even though the rest of the letter is wordprocessed. These parts of the letter, which are standard to all letters and allow you to recognize that a document is a letter, are what is meant by the word *format*.

Formats as Part of the Canadian Business Tradition

The formats you will be using are part of the Canadian tradition in the business and technical workplace. Like other traditions, some of the rules you learn will make sense and others will not. Think of format rules the way you think about rules for setting a table for a meal. It makes sense to have people's plates directly in front of them, since it would be awkward to eat large plates of food off to one side. On the other hand, it would probably be equally logical in Canada to have the fork to the right of the plate as to the left.

So, why do you set the table with the fork to the left? Because that's where Canadian tradition says it should go, and if you don't put the fork there, you'll have a lot of diners complaining that they can't find their forks. If the diners do find their forks, they'll be apt to worry that if you can't set the table right, maybe the food won't be properly cooked either.

Notice that traditions are cultural. In addition, individuals and groups of individuals within a culture may do things differently. Where would you put the chopsticks when setting the table? Do you know how to set the table when there are two different-sized spoons, knives, and forks? If you were training in the hospitality industry, you would learn how to set a table for a banquet, and the conventions of the restaurant and catering industry would determine the rules you would learn. These conventions would in turn be based upon the expectations of the customers of that industry. The conventions of Canadian business and industry, and the expectations of your Canadian readers, will likewise determine the rules you will learn to follow in writing your letters and memos.

GUIDELINE 6:

Use a standard Canadian format when writing your letters and memos.

Letters and Memos

A letter is an external message sent to a reader outside the writer's business or place of work. Because a letter is always sent outside the business, it always includes the full address of the writer and the reader. A memo, short for *memorandum* (the plural form is *memoranda* or *memorandums*), is an internal message sent within a department in a business or a place of work, or sent from one part of the business to another. Thus, while a memo may include such details as the reader's and writer's names, job titles, and department or division names, it does not include either the reader's or the writer's full postal address.

You would write memos to your supervisors, co-workers, and to the people you supervise. You would write letters to other businesses, organizations, and governments, and to outside customers, clients, and the general public. Since letters represent your business to the "outside world," to its customers and potential customers, letters are generally more formal than memos.

Think of a memo as you with your jacket or blazer hanging on the hook behind your door, or over the back of your chair, while you communicate with people who see you daily at work. You're not in your bathing suit under a beach umbrella, but you're not dressed up either. Think of a letter as you wearing your blazer and decorative scarf, or jacket and tie, spruced up to impress, but not overdressed as for a night at the opera or at a rock concert.

You may have seen a "speedy memo" in the workplace. This is a very short memo, which is usually a half-page or less in length. Do not conclude on this basis that a memo can never be more than a page in length. Some memos are two or even three pages long. As you have learned in this chapter, a document is as long as it needs to be to supply your readers with all the information they need to do what you want them to do as a result of your writing. Neither your memos nor your letters should be any longer or shorter than needed for your readers and purpose.

The letters and memos you will be writing in this book are routine. They are written to request information or to give information. They are not sophisticated documents written to persuade readers to do something they wouldn't normally do or to inform readers that you won't be able to do what they've asked you to do. Most memo and letter writing at work is routine. If you take a more advanced course in business and technical writing, and we hope you do, you'll learn how to write persuasive letters and memos, which are often more difficult to write.

Rules for Memos

Include the words "TO," "FROM," "DATE," and "SUBJECT" as shown in the memo you read on the company harassment policy. Beside "TO" and "FROM" include the job titles, as well as the names of, the reader and the writer. If the memo is to all staff in a department, you may write "All Staff" beside "TO." You may initial in ink or sign your name in ink beside your typed name in the "FROM" section, or at the bottom of your memo at the left margin, or in the centre, or at the right margin. Do not write a closing, such as "Sincerely," at the bottom of your memo. Do not begin your memo with a salutation, such as "Dear...."

Rules for Letters

There is more than one way to write a properly formatted business letter. In this book, we use a block letter format with open punctuation because it is used by many businesses in Canada, and we think you will find it easy to learn and use.

For this format, all text—addresses, salutation, subject line and other headings, paragraphs, and complimentary closing—begins at the left-hand margin. All text is single-spaced.

Double-space between each section of the letter. Some businesses triple-space before and after the subject line. Leave four blank lines between the complimentary close and the typed name of the writer to allow adequate space for a signature.

"Open punctuation" usually means just omitting the colon after the salutation ("Dear Mr. Yang") and the comma after the complimentary close ("Sincerely").

Here is a table giving the rules for the parts of a letter using this block letter format:

Table 1.2
Block letter format

part	rules
Writer's address (Inside address)	▪ Your employer may provide company letterhead for you to use for the first page of your letter. Company letterhead is pre-printed and includes at the top the company name, address, and telephone number, and often a special design or advertising logo. If you use company letterhead, don't repeat your address. If your letterhead does not include

your department name, you may type it below the letterhead.

- Do not include the writer's name in the writer's address. Just as you do not include the writer's name, you should also omit the writer's job title.

- Write each item in the address on a separate line with no punctuation, such as commas, at the end of the lines. In the address would appear the department name (optional), company name, street number and street name or rural route address, city and province, and country and postal code (separated from the country by two blank spaces). Include the country only if the reader's address is in a different country.

- Do not abbreviate except for the province. For the province, use the two-letter official Canada Post designation. If you don't include the country, type the postal code after the name of the province. The Canadian postal code does not include a hyphen.

Date	• State the date on which the letter was written.
	• Use the order of month, day, and year, or day, month, and year. Write out the month in full; do not abbreviate the month's name.
Reader's address (Outside address)	• Include the first and last name of the reader.
	• Use a courtesy title: Ms., Mr., Dr., or Rev. If you do not know if your reader is a Ms. or a Mr., omit the courtesy title.
	• Arrange the information in an address from specific to general. On the line following the reader's name, write the reader's job title. The next line is for the reader's division or department. On the line after that, type the company name, and on the following lines, the street address, and city and province.
Salutation	• Use "Dear" and the courtesy title and last name (family name) of your reader. Only use the given and family names (first and last names) together if you don't know if your reader is a Mr. or a Ms.

Subject line	▪ Highlight your subject line by (1) capitalizing the initial letters of the major words; (2) underlining the entire subject line; (3) having it appear in bold; or (4) by typing the entire line in all capital letters.
	▪ You may use the word *Subject* or omit it.
Body of the letter	▪ Begin each of your paragraphs at the left-hand margin and double-space between your paragraphs.
	▪ You may type "...2" flush with the right-hand margin at the bottom of the first page of a two-page letter.
	▪ At the top of the second page of a two-page letter, type the reader's name, the date, and the page number.
	▪ Do not use a postscript (a PS) in a business letter.
Complimentary close	▪ Use a common close such as "Sincerely."
Signature	▪ Sign your name as it appears below in type.
Writer's name and title	▪ Type your name in full. Type your job title below your name.
Reference initials	▪ Flush with the left-hand margin, type in capital letters the initials of the writer and, in lowercase letters, the initials of the typist. If you wrote and typed the letter yourself, don't type in any initials.
Enclosure notation	▪ Include "Enclosure" if there is an enclosure with your letter. You may use the abbreviation "Enc."
	▪ Type the number of enclosures if there are more than one: "Enclosures (2)." You may also identify the enclosure if you wish: "Enclosure: cheque for $5,468.94."
Copy notation	▪ Include "CC" (courtesy copy) and the names and job titles of those also receiving copies of your letter. List them in order of importance according to their positions in the company or in alphabetical order.

Here is a letter in the full block format with open punctuation. The parts are labelled.

FULL BLOCK WITH OPEN PUNCTUATION

Writer's address	RR #2 S-19 C-45 Belleville, ON K8N 4Z2
Date	May 15, 199—
Reader's address	Ms. Fatima Saad Manager Product Development Interactive Technologies 451 Main Street Winnipeg, MB R3C 2G1
Salutation	Dear Ms. Saad
Subject line	**Subject: Acceptance of Your Offer of Employment**
Body of letter	I am pleased to accept a full-time position as a Technologist in Product Development with Interactive Technologies. Enclosed is Form 210A, which I completed as you requested. As we arranged over the telephone, I will be reporting for my first day on the job at 9 a.m. on Monday, June 1. I am looking forward to working for you, and if you have any questions or information for me before Monday, please write or call me at (613) 967-2808.
Complimentary close	Sincerely
Signature	*Réjean Côté*
Writer's name and title (if appropriate)	Réjean Côté
Enclosure notation	Enc.

Here is the same letter in two other formats you may see in business: modified block with mixed punctuation, and the new simplified format.

MODIFIED BLOCK WITH MIXED PUNCTUATION

RR #2 S-19 C-45
Belleville, ON K8N 4Z2

May 15, 199—

Ms. Fatima Saad
Manager
Product Development
Interactive Technologies
451 Main Street
Winnipeg, MB R3C 2G1

Dear Ms. Saad:

Subject: Acceptance of Your Offer of Employment

I am pleased to accept a full-time position as a Technologist in Product Development with Interactive Technologies.

Enclosed is Form 210A, which I completed as you requested. As we arranged over the telephone, I will be reporting for my first day on the job at 9 a.m. on Monday, June 1.

I am looking forward to working with you, and if you have any questions or information for me before Monday, please write or call me at (613) 967-2808.

Sincerely

Réjean Côté

Réjean Côté
Enc.

SIMPLIFIED FORMAT

RR #2 S-19 C-45
Belleville, ON K8N 4Z2

May 15, 199—

Ms. Fatima Saad
Manager
Product Development
Interactive Technologies
451 Main Street
Winnipeg, MB R3C 2G1

ACCEPTANCE OF YOUR OFFER OF EMPLOYMENT

Ms. Saad, I am pleased to accept a full-time position as a Technologist in Product Development with Interactive Technologies.

Enclosed is Form 210A, which I completed as you requested. As we arranged over the telephone, I will be reporting for my first day on the job at 9 a.m. on Monday, June 1.

I am looking forward to working with you, and if you have any questions or information for me before Monday, please write or call me at (613) 967-2808.

Réjean Côté

REJEAN COTE
Enc.

SUBJECT LINES FOR YOUR LETTERS AND MEMOS

Above the text of a letter or a memo, a **subject line** tells the reader what the message is about. The subject line is the title of your message. If you don't include one, your reader has no idea why you wrote the message. If you don't write a *good* subject line, your message may be passed to the wrong reader, and it may be wrongly filed.

Be specific when you write a subject line. Imagine the reaction at a lumber company to a letter headed "Lumber." Imagine the effect on a safety officer of seeing a memo headed "Safety." These subject lines are wastes of time. Here is an unclear subject line to study:

Subject: Noise

If you saw this at the top of a memo at work, you might guess that the message was

- an inspection report on office conditions
- a technical solution to a noise problem
- a complaint about talkative workers
- a review of new Workers' Compensation Board (WCB) regulations.

The writer knew what the message was but didn't take the time to explain:

Subject: Likely Disturbance from Machine Testing

Be concise when you write a subject line. Don't write a sentence: Subject: Staff are using vans without permission. Use a fragment or phrase: Subject: Unauthorized Use of Vans.

You may write "Subject" or simply write and underline the phrase. You may have seen the word *Re* at the beginning of a subject line or in a business letter or memo. We suggest that you use the word *Subject* instead because *Re* is a Latin word, and you should avoid Latin in everyday writing. You may say what kind of message it is by beginning with words like the following:

Subject: Request for…

Subject: Invitation to…

Subject: Report on…

Subject: Proposal to…

Subject: Reminder to…

Subject: Warning to…

Recommendation for… .

Avoid negative subject lines such as Subject: Refusal of… and Subject: Complaint about… .

GUIDELINE 7:

Give your memos and letters subject lines that are both specific and concise. Be positive: avoid negative subject lines.

Practice

Write a subject line to suit each of the following messages.

1. The procedure for signing out the office notebook computer has changed. As of June 1, all staff will be expected to start following this new procedure. Your message tells staff about the new procedure.

SUBJECT: _____

_____

2. The office where you work has just had a computer printer installed. The people in the office are now complaining about how much noise the printer makes. They say it gives them headaches, even though the sales representative assured them they wouldn't notice the noise. The sales representative had agreed (in writing) to install a special oak sound cover over the printer free of charge if there were problems. Now that there have been problems, you must write the computer company to ask them to install the sound cover.

SUBJECT: _____

_____

3. Recently you inspected the product testing station off the packing area. Two radiators were not working, even when the thermostat was turned up. Also, the air conditioning system has loose baffles that vibrate easily. The work needed to correct these problems is minor. You leave a memo for the maintenance engineer who does this work.

SUBJECT: _____

_____

4. Your Communication class is learning how to prepare a résumé and letter of application and how to participate in a job interview. You decide to invite someone from industry to speak to your class. You had a very good speaker from industry last term, who spoke on communication skills needed on the job, so you decide to invite her back to speak on the hiring process.

SUBJECT: _____

_____

5. Your wood products manufacturing class went on a field trip to a local plywood mill. You really enjoyed the tour the company gave you. The company took you through the entire production line, showed you a video, held a question-and-answer session, and even gave you a free lunch. You decide to write the mill a letter thanking them for the tour.

SUBJECT: _____

_____

6. You've been having problems with the cleaning agent you've been using to clean the vats and counters in your fish-packing plant. You decide to talk to your chemical supply company about switching cleaning agents. First, you need a report from the supervisor on all the problems with the cleaning solution you are currently using. You write your supervisor a memo asking for the report.

SUBJECT: _____

_____

7. You circulate a memo to all staff in a warehouse. You are fed up with complaints and frequent incidents stemming from staff playing with, and sometimes racing, the company fork-lift trucks. You intend to discipline any offenders in the future. This memo publicly warns everybody.

   SUBJECT: _____

   _____

8. You write a letter to a cleaning contractor whose crew spilled chemicals and scratched paintwork on their last visit to your office suite. This is a letter of complaint.

   SUBJECT: _____

   _____

9. You write a memo to a senior manager. The manager has decided to put all company delivery drivers under the supervision of the sales manager instead of the shipping manager who has overseen them until now. You are sure this will be a disastrous change, and you want the senior manager to reconsider.

   SUBJECT: _____

   _____

10. You write a letter to a petro-chemical company. You are a member of a residents' association; many members have complained about an increase in smoke and smell from the plant. You want to visit the company with your committee members to meet the manager and to tell her of your feelings.

    SUBJECT: _____

    _____

INFORMAL AND FORMAL REPORTS

Informal Reports

Reports are organized, objective presentations of factual information. Informal reports are usually written in letter or memo format and are usually shorter than ten pages.

An example of an informal report you might write at work would be a memo to your supervisor telling her the results of your investigation into the possible causes of the death of all the bacteria you'd been using to digest your pulp mill's effluent. Another example would be a memo report you would be asked to write to your supervisor after you had had an accident with the company car.

An example of an informal letter report would be a proposal you might write in a letter to a potential customer who managed a fish-processing plant. The proposal would describe how your product could be used to clean fish waste from the plant equipment.

In your informal reports, you would put in the first paragraph your main idea and the precise action you wished your reader to take.

Formal Reports

Formal reports are usually ten pages or longer. Rather than being written as memos or letters, they are bound documents similar in appearance to books with title pages, tables of contents, and several other sections. They are accompanied by cover memos or letters, which are clipped to the outside of the report folders.

When you arrange the information in a formal report, you should place the main idea *and* any recommended action at the front.

When you write a formal report, it is almost always *at the request* of someone. Even before you begin to write, the person is expecting some kind of answer. The answer may be an investigation, a comparison or a feasibility study; for example, the roof on an underground parking garage has collapsed, and a report is needed to find the cause and recommend ways to prevent the roof from collapsing again. The subsequent report may be thirty pages long or three thousand pages long. What do your readers most need to know? Are they happy to read thirty or three thousand pages before finding the answer?

Many writers are doubly reluctant to use the strategy of placing the main idea and recommended action at the front. Again, that detective-story attitude may discourage them from revealing the news at the beginning. Remind yourself that you are not expected, at work, to write suspense novels. Write a summary no longer than one page that includes the recommended action, and place your summary immediately after the title page.

Outlines for Formal Reports

Here is a suggested outline for a simple formal report:

1. Title page
2. Summary
3. Contents list
4. Introduction
5. Conclusions and recommendations
6. Main body of report
7. Appendices.

Some companies follow a more traditional pattern:

1. Title page
2. Summary
3. Contents list
4. Introduction
5. Main body of report
6. Conclusions and recommendations
7. Appendices.

Thus, in both formal and informal reports you would put your main idea first as you do in your letters and memos.

REVIEW QUESTIONS

In your own words, define the following five key terms and answer the three questions:

PURPOSE: _____

_____

_____

READER NEEDS: _____

_____

_____

OUTLINE: _____

_____

_____

MAIN IDEA: _____

_____

_____

MAIN IDEA SENTENCE: _____

_____

_____

1. Why do you think it's important to begin by defining your purpose?

_____

_____

_____

2. What are the benefits of defining your readers?

_____

_____

_____

3. What is the most effective order to use for your memos and letters?

_____

_____

PRACTICE WRITING ASSIGNMENT

Karen Klugholz received the following notice in the mail at home:

To the Residents of:

Elm Road to Oak Lane
Lakeshore Road
Maple Road to Birch Lane

You are invited to attend a town meeting on October 5, 199—, at 10 a.m., in the Cobourg Council Chambers, 55 King Street West, Cobourg, to discuss the following two items:

1. whether the town should erect three-way stop signs at the intersection of Elm, Lakeshore, and Maple streets

2. beach party control at the Lakeshore Road beach.

If you wish to speak on either item at the meeting, please send us your request in writing by October 1, and we will put you on the agenda.

If you are unable to attend the meeting, please send us your comments in writing by October 5, addressed to the Public Works Superintendent, Mr. Wilbert Wok.

Wilbert Wok

Wilbert Wok
Public Works Superintendent

Now read the letter Karen wrote to the Public Works Superintendent.

501 Lakeshore Road
Cobourg, ON K9A 1S4

September 14, 199—

Mr. Wilbert Wok
Public Works Superintendent
Town of Cobourg
55 King Street West
Cobourg, ON K9A 2M2

Dear Mr. Wok

I understand from the notice I received that residents of Elm Road to Oak Lane, Lakeshore Road, and Maple Road to Birch Lane may speak at a town meeting on October 5, regarding either the three-way stop signs proposed for the intersection of Elm, Lakeshore, and Maple, or beach party control at the Lakeshore Road beach.

I happen to live on Lakeshore Road, which will definitely be affected by the proposed stop signs, and I feel very strongly about this matter. That's why I want to make sure I get to speak at the town meeting regarding the proposed stop signs.

The notice sent to me at my above address stated that persons interested in speaking at the meeting should send you requests in writing to speak. I suppose you'll want to know which issue I want to speak on, so you'll know which part of the agenda to put me on.

I can't say often enough that I'm strongly in favour of having those three stop signs erected. I think that the people who live in the neighbourhood need to be listened to for a change. The people who live on my street are getting sick and tired of everyone's speeding through our street on the way to the mall, which I never felt should have been built in the first place. Our nice downtown with little shops used to be good enough for people, but not anymore. Having no stop signs might help those people get to the mall faster, but what about the neighbourhood children and pets who could get hurt by all those speeding cars? And what about all the noise? The faster the traffic, the louder it is. We need to slow those cars down to produce quieter, safer neighbourhoods.

By the way, I don't have anything to say about beach parties. I live at the other end of the road, and that beach is fifty-seven steps (I counted them!) below the road, so I can never hear any noise from the beach. Maybe the people who live closer to the beach are bothered by beach parties. I don't know.

I'm sure all the people on my street will be at your meeting to speak for the proposal. You said I had to get this letter to you by October 1. Well, Canada Post ought to be able to get you this letter in two weeks. I also want to make sure I see the agenda for the meeting, so I know what's going on and when I'll be speaking.

Sincerely

Karen Klugholz

Karen Klugholz

Note: Residents in small towns and large cities often request to speak at special meetings or regular council meetings on issues that affect them. The information a town or city requires to put you on the agenda to speak varies, and you should read the notice of meeting very carefully or call the town or city clerk's office to find out what you need to do if you want to speak at the meeting, or if you can't attend the meeting and want to comment in writing. Handling such requests for information from the public is an important part of the clerk's job, and staff will be glad to give you the information.

Study Questions for the Practice Writing Assignment

1. What is the writer's purpose in the letter you read?

_____

_____

2. Does the writer express that purpose?

_____

_____

3. Why or why not?

_____

_____

4. What action does the writer specify?

_____

_____

Fill in the following Writing Plan Sheet and then rewrite the letter. Remember to include a subject line telling your reader what your letter is about.

Writing Plan Sheet for the Practice Writing Assignment

Purpose

1. What is my purpose?

_____

_____

2. What results do I want?

_____

_____

Reader Needs

3. Who is my reader?

_____

_____

4. What things will my reader need to know?

_____

_____

5. What action do I want my reader to take?

_____

_____

Outline

Main Idea: _____

_____

Details: _____

_____

Main Idea: _____

_____

Details: _____

_____

Main Idea: _____

_____

Details: _____

_____

Now compare your letter with the suggested rewrite.

SUGGESTED REWRITE OF UNPLANNED LETTER TO THE TOWN OF COBOURG

501 Lakeshore Road
Cobourg, ON K9A 1S4

September 14, 199—

Mr. Wilbert Wok
Public Works Superintendent
Town of Cobourg
55 King Street West
Cobourg, ON K9A 2M2

Dear Mr. Wok

Subject: Request to Speak at the Town Meeting

I would like to speak at the meeting on October 5.

The item on the agenda I would like to address is the proposal for three-way stop signs at the intersection at Elm, Lakeshore, and Maple.

Would you please send me a copy of the agenda before the meeting?

Sincerely

Karen Klugholz

Karen Klugholz

Notice how the writer uses the three parts of her letter to express three important ideas: (1) the writer states her **purpose** for writing; (2) the writer answers the **reader's needs**; and (3) the writer requests a specific **action**.

Because this letter is so short, you might be tempted to write a one-paragraph letter. Don't. Help your readers by keeping these three separate pieces of information separate on the page. Your reader may want to quickly check the date or the topic. Having these items in separate paragraphs makes that task easier for your readers. Your readers may also want to circle your request for an agenda in the last paragraph as a reminder to themselves or someone else to get back to you. Don't worry that your paragraphs will be too short. Your paragraphs may be as short as one typed line or as long as seven lines.

QUESTION SHEET

List any questions you have about this chapter:

Questions

_____

_____

_____

_____

_____

_____

_____

_____

_____

_____

_____

_____

Answers

_____

_____

_____

_____

_____

_____

_____

_____

_____

_____

_____

_____

_____

◢ EXERCISES

Exercise 1: Using Language that Includes All Readers

You've learned the importance of picturing your reader while you write. You've also learned how to correct for any prejudices that might prevent you from forming an accurate picture of your reader. For example, we discussed the importance, in the case of the VISA letter, of realizing that the reader, the customer service representative, could be either a man or a woman.

To correct for prejudices, you'll also have to correct your language. In the case of the VISA letter, you would have to change "Dear Sir" to "Dear Customer Service Representative," or omit the salutation, or, if possible, find out your reader's name and use it.

This exercise will give you practice in changing your language so it is free of prejudice. This exercise has two parts: Using Pronouns that Include All Readers, and Using Job Titles and Other Special Terms from the Work World to Include All Readers.

Using Pronouns that Include All Readers

To use pronouns effectively in your writing, you need to be able to avoid errors in pronoun agreement.

A singular pronoun (he, she, it; his, her, its; him, her, it) is used to refer to a singular noun (Alberto, Nancy, keyboard). A plural pronoun (they, their, them) is used to refer to a plural noun (keyboards). Which pronoun correctly completes the following sentence?

The marketing department met all (its/their) deadlines for the month.

The correct answer is *its*. The noun "department" is singular, so the pronoun should also be singular.

Exercise A

Circle the correct pronoun in the following sentences. Also, draw a line under the noun that the pronoun is replacing.

1. We had to repair the equipment (ourself/ourselves).
2. Our swimming club is having (their/its) annual banquet this weekend.
3. Two people in the group discussed (his/their) assignments with the instructor.
4. The students complained that Professor Kelly spoke too quickly to (them/him).
5. The trainees were instructed to finish the programming (themself/themselves).

Exercise B

Use a pronoun to complete the following sentences.

1. Not one of the new fathers will be returning to ___their___ job next term.
2. Everyone in the women's group has volunteered some of ___their___ time for the fundraising event.
3. Coordinators are responsible for circulating the report in ___their___ departments.
4. People hiking the trail in Mont Orford Provincial Park must carry everything in _____ backpacks.
5. The door squeaks because _____ hinges need oiling.

When you use pronouns to refer to nouns, remember to replace any pronouns that inaccurately exclude women or men.

Use the masculine pronoun (he, his, him) only when you know that the person the pronoun stands for is a male. Do not use the masculine pronoun to stand for males and females. Use the feminine pronoun (she, her, her) only when you know that the person the pronoun stands for is a female. Do not use the feminine pronoun to stand for females and males.

For example, write

David Chiu handed in his vacation request before the end of the month.

You know David is a man, so you use the masculine pronoun.
Do not write

Each employee should hand in his vacation request before the end of the month.

An employee may be either a man or woman, so you should not use only the masculine pronoun. To correct the language in this sentence, you can

1. **use a plural pronoun** (they, their, them), if possible:

Employees should hand in their vacation requests before the end of the month.

2. **use a "you" pronoun**, if appropriate:

You should hand in your vacation requests by the end of the month.

3. **rephrase your sentence to leave out the pronoun**, if possible. You may have to add "a" or "an" or "the."

Each employee should hand in a vacation request by the end of the month.

4. **use the "inferred you."** This approach would be suitable for giving directions, steps, or instructions. Use only present tense verbs.

Hand in vacation requests by the end of the month.

5. **use "her or his" (or "his or her")**. This solution is only recommended when no other solution is available and thus is not recommended for this example.

Each employee should hand in her or his vacation request before the end of the month.

Many people accept the following use of the plural pronoun to stand for a singular noun that refers to either a woman or a man:

Each employee should hand in their vacation request before the end of the month.

However, many others still consider any use of a plural pronoun to refer to a singular noun to be incorrect. Thus, you would be wise to change the noun to a plural whenever possible.

Exercise C

Now rewrite the following sentences to ensure that they use language that includes all readers. After you've made the necessary changes, check that singular pronouns refer to singular nouns and plural pronouns refer to plural nouns.

1. Each division head should meet with his employees to choose a coordinator for our fundraising campaign.

   _____

   _____

2. The coordinator should have some experience in organizing fundraising activities. He should also have leadership skills and enjoy working as part of a team.

   _____

   _____

3. If anyone is interested in volunteering for this position, please have him call me or e-mail me.

_____

_____

4. The person you select should be willing to work some weekends and evenings. He'll be given time off at the end of the campaign.

_____

_____

5. Let's hope everyone does his best to help make this year's campaign a success.

_____

_____

Exercise D

Now try rewriting the following sentences to ensure that they use language that includes all readers. Use _appropriate_ methods to correct the language. You may use plural pronouns or rephrase sentences to leave out the pronouns. The first sentence is done for you.

1. Each department supervisor is responsible for developing a recycling program for his department.

   Department supervisors are responsible for developing recycling programs for their departments.

2. I propose we hire an additional full-time staff person. His job will be to collect and prepare recyclables for shipment.

   _____

   _____

3. If you know anyone who would be suitable for the position, please have him call me at Ext. 7185.

   _____

   _____

4. If the average person would simply recycle his morning newspaper, we would cut down household waste by 10 percent.

   _____

   _____

5. While many of the items used in a hospital ward cannot be recycled, each head nurse can ensure that the discarded office paper in her ward is recycled.

   _____

   _____

Using Job Titles and Other Special Terms from the Work World to Include All Readers

Job titles such as "customer service representative" and "customer sales representative" are gender neutral, that is, they do not express any prejudice that the person in the job is more likely to be a man or a woman. In contrast, job titles such as "service*man*" and "sales*man*" reflect the prejudicial assumption that all service and sales representatives are men.

Change the following terms to correct for prejudice. The first one is done for you.

1. businessmen *business people* _____
2. cleaning lady ___*Cleaning person*_____
3. chairman ___*chair person — chair*_____
4. fireman ___*Figth fighters*_____
5. girl at the front desk ___*recepciouist*_____
6. mailman ___*mail courier*_____
7. man the equipment ___*operators*_____
8. managers and their wives ___*manager and their partners*_____
9. man hours ___*people hours*_____
10. woman lawyer ___*lawyer*_____
11. manning the office ___*staff in the office*_____
12. Workmen's Compensation ___*Workers Compensation.*_____

Exercise 2: Making Your Purpose Clear

Before you start to write, you need to know your purpose. As you've learned, it's a good idea to decide why you're writing, and to know what results you expect from your writing, *before* you write your letter or memo. You also know you should **state your purpose at the beginning of a letter or memo if possible.** In the case of the letter to the public works superintendent, for example, you had to revise the first sentence of the letter to make it clear that the writer wanted to speak at the meeting.

This exercise will give you practice in learning to write clear purpose statements. Two different purpose statements appear below, along with brief descriptions of the situations that led the people to write the letters.

This exercise has two parts. First, you and your partner will be discussing answers to questions. Then, you'll be rewriting two purpose statements by yourself.

Discussing Answers to Questions

Read each purpose statement. Then discuss the answers with a partner or with the other people in your group.

1. Ying Chang bought the latest Celine Dion CD at A & B Sound last month; she charged it to her VISA card. When she received her VISA statement, she noticed she had been charged twice for the same CD. She phoned VISA to explain the error, but the VISA representative told her she would have to write a letter to VISA's Toronto office.

Purpose Statement: When I spoke with you on the phone today, I explained that there was a mistake in my VISA bill, and you asked me to write this letter.

a. Is the purpose clearly stated? Do you know what the writer wants the reader to do?

_____

_____

_____

b. Should any of the information be omitted or used in another part of the letter? Should any information be added?

_____

_____

_____

c. What will Ying's reader need to know *first*? (What does she want her reader to do?)

_____

_____

_____

2. Martin Grabowski is planning to attend the Gateway Institute of Technology next September, so he's writing to Admissions to get information about Gateway's programs.

Purpose Statement: My name is Martin. I would like to study at the Gateway Institute of Technology next September because I heard from my friends that Gateway is a well-known institution.

a. Is the purpose clearly stated? Do you know what the writer wants the reader to do?

_____

_____

_____

b. Should any of the information be omitted or used in another part of the letter? Should any information be added?

_____

_____

_____

c. What does the reader of Martin's letter need to know *first*? (What does he want his reader to do?)

_____

_____

_____

Rewriting Purpose Statements

By yourself, rewrite each of the purpose statements in the spaces below.

1. Ying's Purpose Statement:

    _____

    _____

2. Martin's Purpose Statement:

    _____

    _____

Exercise 3: Defining Your Reader and Your Purpose

This exercise will help you learn to plan *before* you write by helping you define your reader *and* your purpose.

Below are descriptions of three different situations that would require you to write. Read each description and answer the questions.

1. You live in Stephenville. You bought a camera at a specialty store in St. John's. Now your camera's broken. Luckily, your camera is still under warranty. You decide to send the camera back to the store where you bought it, so the store can either fix it or replace it.

    a. Who is your reader?

        _____

        _____

    b. What will your reader need to know first? (In other words: What is your purpose? What do you want your reader to do?)

        _____

        _____

    c. What other things will your reader need to be told?

        _____

        _____

2. A worker in your office spilled a cup of coffee on one of the computer keyboards and ruined it. You want to write to the workers in the office reminding them not to eat and drink at their computer work stations.

    a. Who is your reader?

        _____

        _____

b. What will your reader need to know first? (In other words: What is your purpose? What do you want your reader to do?)

_____

_____

c. What other things will your reader need to be told?

_____

_____

3. You've been subpoenaed to be a witness in a trial. You need to write your manager asking for three days off work to attend the trial.

a. Who is your reader?

_____

_____

b. What will your reader need to know first? (In other words: What is your purpose? What do you want your reader to do?)

_____

_____

c. What other things will your reader need to be told?

_____

_____

Exercise 4: Using a Standard Canadian Format for Your Letters and Memos

This exercise will give you a chance to practise what you've learned about the differences between a letter and a memo and about letter and memo formats.

The exercise has two parts: Choosing a Letter or Memo, and Spotting Letter and Memo Format Errors

Choosing a Letter or Memo

Read each situation below and decide if you would write a letter or a memo. Choose only one option for each situation.

1. You're a graduate in Financial Management, and your first job is managing the financial records and budget for a non-profit society. With the approval of the society's executive director, you've made changes to the petty cash policy (_petty cash_ is a small fund used to pay minor office expenses). You need to inform all staff of the new policy.

2. You are a quality control supervisor in a sawmill. Your mill is interested in buying a new computerized control system. You've heard that another mill has already

installed such a system, and you decide to write to them to ask permission to view the system in operation.

3. You are an occupational health nurse. You need to replace the office audiometer (a piece of equipment used to test hearing) and decide to write for a price quotation from three different suppliers.

4. You manage your own business: an environmental testing laboratory. At your next staff meeting, you want to review the laboratory procedures for handling soil samples. You want all staff to come to the meeting prepared to discuss any changes they'd like to make to the procedures.

Spotting Letter and Memo Format Errors

Exercise A

The following memo contains five errors in memo format. Can you spot the errors? Correct them by crossing out errors, writing any changes on the memo, and supplying any missing information.

TO: All Staff

DATE: January 2, 199—

Dear Everybody,

Please come to our office recycling fair and find out about our new program, "No Garbage In, No Garbage Out."

    Date: Friday, November 10th

    Time: the lunch hour (12 to 1)

    Place: the main lobby

We'll be giving away great "green" door prizes, including our new "Save a Tree" stamp to encourage photocopying on both sides of the paper. See you there.

Sincerely,

Marilyn Jazebowski

Marilyn Jazebowski

Exercise B

The following letter in full block with open punctuation contains five errors in letter format. Can you spot the errors? Correct them by crossing them out, writing your changes on the letter, and supplying any missing information.

James MacDonald

70 Sullivan Street
Toronto, ON
M5T 1C2

Ms. Raminder Dosanjh
Industrial Relations Manager
Perfection Plywood Mill
14352 Louden Park
Brantford, ON

Dear Ms. Raminder

Tour of Your Plywood Mill by Valley College Wood Products Students

On behalf of the first-year wood products technology students at Valley College, I would like to thank you for giving us a tour of the Perfection Plywood Mill on October 24, 199—.

Please give our special thanks to Herb Wendt, Terry Hewgill, and Allan Liu, who did excellent jobs conducting the tour groups. They took the time to answer all our questions while showing us the entire processing area.

As a former sawmill relief supervisor, I have firsthand knowledge of the difficulties that handling such a large tour of students can present to a company. This knowledge makes me appreciate even more the effort you and your staff took to guarantee us such a successful tour.

Once again, thank you for allowing us to tour your mill.

Sincerely

James MacDonald

James MacDonald
Class Representative

P.S. Thank you also for the excellent luncheon you served us. The egg-salad sandwiches and the carrot sticks were great.

Exercise C

The following letter in the simplified format contains five errors in letter format. Can you spot the errors? Correct them by crossing them out, writing your changes on the letter, and supplying any missing information.

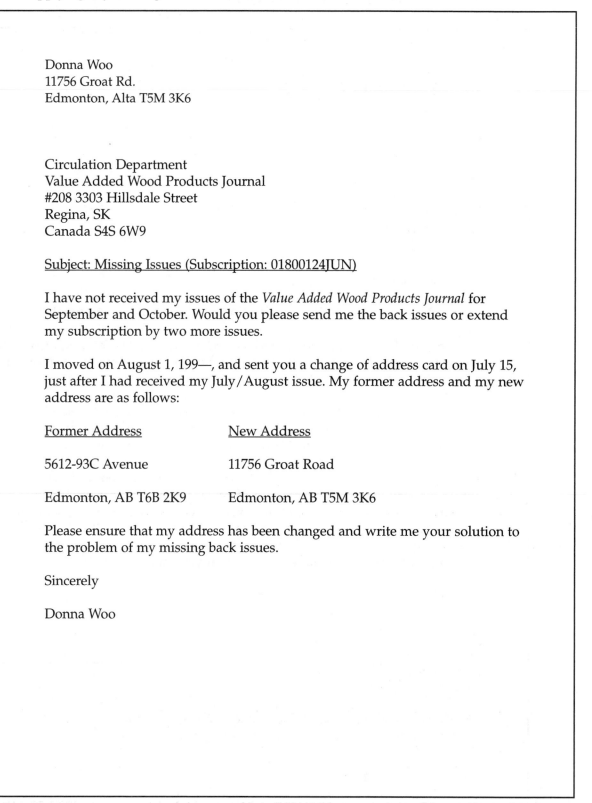

Donna Woo
11756 Groat Rd.
Edmonton, Alta T5M 3K6

Circulation Department
Value Added Wood Products Journal
#208 3303 Hillsdale Street
Regina, SK
Canada S4S 6W9

Subject: Missing Issues (Subscription: 01800124JUN)

I have not received my issues of the *Value Added Wood Products Journal* for September and October. Would you please send me the back issues or extend my subscription by two more issues.

I moved on August 1, 199—, and sent you a change of address card on July 15, just after I had received my July/August issue. My former address and my new address are as follows:

Former Address   New Address

5612-93C Avenue   11756 Groat Road

Edmonton, AB T6B 2K9   Edmonton, AB T5M 3K6

Please ensure that my address has been changed and write me your solution to the problem of my missing back issues.

Sincerely

Donna Woo

Exercise 5: Writing a Main-Idea-First Memo

The Annual Company Picnic

Balminder Moore is a technologist working for Short Circuit, a small electronics company. The company has twenty employees. Five of the twenty employees have been hired in the last six months, while the other fifteen have been with the company since it was founded two years ago.

The company is having its annual summer picnic at the company president's house on Lake Simcoe. Usually all the employees attend the picnic, and although the picnic is at the president's house, employees volunteer to help organize the picnic and to bring food. Balminder volunteered to write the invitations to the picnic. Here's the memo she wrote:

TO: All Short Circuit Staff

FROM: Balminder Moore, Electronic Technologist

DATE: June 15, 199—

The picnic is at the president's house this year. Bring your bathing suits, since the president has a swimming pool.

It's on Saturday, July 7th, so I hope we'll have sunny weather. We'll have the picnic rain or shine, but leave your bathing suits at home if there's thunder and lightning. No matter what the weather is, sign up at Paul's desk to say you're coming and to say what food you're bringing. Remember that great lasagna Sylvia made last year?

Our picnic is a family event, so bring your wives and children. The picnic starts at 2 p.m. and ends at 9 p.m. Paul has a map at his desk if you need to know how to get there. Oh, by the way, you should also sign up at Paul's desk if you need a ride to the picnic.

The president's picnic is an annual event and everyone is welcome. If you don't come, you're fired—just joking! Just tell Paul by June 30th if you're able to come and how many people you'll be bringing, so we know how many people to expect.

B. M.

When Balminder re-read what she'd written, she realized that while the important details were all there, they seemed all mixed up and in the wrong order. Balminder also felt she could have left out some of the details.

She decided to follow the guidelines in her book on writing successfully. First she would plan her message, and then she would make an outline.

Working alone, you can fill in this plan sheet for Balminder:

Writing Plan Sheet

Purpose

1. What is my purpose?

_____

_____

2. What results do I want?

_____

_____

Reader Needs

3. Who is my reader?

_____

_____

4. What things will my reader need to know?

_____

_____

5. What action do I want my reader to take?

_____

_____

Outline

Main Idea

_____

_____

Details

_____

_____

Main Idea

_____

_____

Details

_____

_____

Main Idea

_____

_____

Details

_____

_____

In small groups of three or four students, share your plan sheets. Have each person read aloud her or his answer for each section of the plan sheet and compare answers. If another student has a different answer from yours, change your answer only if the student is able to convince you that you're wrong by referring to the guidelines and examples in this chapter.

Then, individually write the memo. Include a subject line that tells your reader what your memo is about.

In your small group, place each student's memo at the centre of the table, one memo at a time, and evaluate each memo according to the following checklist.

Checklist for Evaluating the Memo

1. Is the purpose stated at the beginning of the memo, in the first sentence? Does the first sentence say what the writer wants the reader to do?
2. Are all readers included? Has the writer been careful not to use language that would exclude any readers?
3. Does the memo answer all the reader's questions? Does the memo tell the reader what, when, where, why, and how?
4. Does each paragraph begin with a main idea sentence?
5. Does each paragraph contain only the details that follow logically from its main idea sentence?
6. Does the memo include only the information the reader needs or wants, so the memo contains no unnecessary details?
7. Does the memo end with a request for a specific action?
8. Is the English correct? Circle any errors in the English.

Finally, revise your memo based on the checklist.

Exercise 6: Writing a Main-Idea-First Letter

A Visit to the United States

Jong Jen Yuen moved to Canada from Hong Kong just over a year ago. He lives in Kamloops, BC, where he has been studying English full-time for six months. A few of his classmates are driving to Seattle, Washington, during the Christmas vacation and have invited him along. He'd love to visit the United States—he's never been farther south than White Rock, BC.

The last time Jong Jen got an invitation to travel to the United States, he didn't have an entry visa, so he couldn't go. He asks several classmates for advice about how to get a visa and gets a number of different answers. One classmate says, "Just send a copy of your landed immigrant papers to the U.S. Consulate." Another, from Mexico, tells him: "You don't need papers; just get a letter from the college saying you're a full-time student." Jong Jen hears of one student whose visa application was denied because her grades were too low.

He decides to write a letter to the U.S. Consulate to find out how to obtain an entry visa. Now read the letter he wrote.

516-1697
Greenfield Avenue
Kamloops, BC
V2B 4N5

October 10, 199—

Vice Consul
Non-Immigrant Visa Section
United States Consulate General
1095 West Pender Street
Vancouver, BC V6C 1J6

Dear Vice Consul

Subject: A Trip to the United States

My name is Jong Jen Yuen. I moved to Canada from Hong Kong in August 1996.
For the first six months, I lived in Edmonton, where my aunt lives, but it was
too cold there, so I moved to Kamloops. I've been studying English full-time at
the University College of the Cariboo for six months.

Some of my friends at the college are driving to Seattle during the Christmas
vacation, and they've invited me along. I'd love to see the United States. I know
I need an entry visa before I go, but I'm not sure what information you need
before you can process my application. Is it true that you sometimes deny visa
applications if a student has poor grades? Do you need a letter from the college?

Could you please send me a list of the documents you require in order to
process my application. I also need to know how long I can stay in the U.S. and
the cost of a visa. Will I need to come to Vancouver for an interview, or can I just
send everything in the mail?

Please send me this information by the end of October, so I'll be able to get my
visa before Christmas.

Sincerely

Jong Jen Yuen

Jong Jen Yuen

Note: To be eligible for an entry visa into the U.S., immigrant students have to show evidence that they've been studying in Canada for six months. If you're working in Canada, you need to show proof of your employment. Canadian citizens don't need an entry visa to visit the U.S. Visa requests are handled by staff in the Non-Immigrant Visa Section; the letter doesn't need to be addressed to a particular person.

You're visiting some friends at the University College of the Cariboo for the weekend; because you've studied how to write effective letters, Jong Jen asks you to read his letter before he mails it. After reading the letter, you see that he could make his enquiry clearer. He's included all the important details, but they are in the wrong order. You feel he also could have omitted a few unnecessary details.

Following the guidelines in this chapter, you decide to first plan the message and then make an outline.

Writing Plan Sheet

Purpose

1. What is my purpose?

_____

_____

2. What results do I want?

_____

_____

Reader Needs

3. Who is my reader?

_____

_____

4. What things will my reader need to know?

_____

_____

5. What action do I want my reader to take?

_____

_____

Outline

Main Idea

_____

_____

Details

_____

_____

Main Idea

_____

_____

Details

_____

_____

Main Idea

_____

_____

Details

_____

_____

In small groups of three or four students, share your plan sheets. Have each person read aloud her or his answer for each section of the plan sheet and compare answers. If another student has a different answer from yours, change your answer only if the student is able to convince you that you're wrong by referring to the guidelines and examples in this chapter.

Then, individually write the letter. Include a subject line that tells your reader what your letter is about.

In your small group, place each student's letter at the centre of the table, one letter at a time, and evaluate each letter according to the following checklist.

Checklist for Evaluating the Letter

1. Is the purpose stated at the beginning of the letter, in the first sentence? Does the first sentence say what the writer wants the reader to do?
2. Are all readers included? Has the writer been careful not to use language that would exclude any readers?
3. Does the letter answer all the reader's questions? Does the letter tell the reader what, when, where, why, and how?
4. Does each paragraph begin with a main idea sentence?
5. Does each paragraph contain only the details that follow logically from its main idea sentence?

6. Does the letter include only the information the reader needs or wants, so the letter contains no unnecessary details?

7. Does the letter end with a request for a specific action?

8. Is the English correct? Circle any errors in the English.

   Finally, revise your letter based on the checklist.

2

PUTTING YOUR MAIN IDEA FIRST IN EVERY SENTENCE

All the cultures we have experienced have their overly official languages that people use when they are anxious to impress the authorities; for example, whether in Berlin or Vancouver, I would say to my friend, "My pick-up truck was stolen from my driveway last night," whereas to the police I might say, "The vehicle that was parked in the driveway last night was last seen by myself at that time."

Often, people are tempted to use this same overly official language in the classroom and in the workplace to impress teachers, supervisors, and customers. However, in our experience, most readers would be much happier if writers used a friendly, direct approach, only slightly more careful and more formal than that of their everyday speech. In this chapter you will learn how to impress your readers with straightforward sentences.

Learning Outcomes

Communication Outcomes

When you finish this chapter, you will be able to

- use active sentences for most business and technical writing
- know when to use passive sentences in your writing
- explain how the use of active or passive voice can determine the tone of your writing
- write sentences that tell your reader what your sentence is about in the first few words.

Language Outcomes

When you finish this chapter, you will be able to

- identify sentences as either active or passive
- use correct forms and word order in your active and passive sentences
- revise passive sentences to make them active, and revise active sentences to make them passive, as appropriate
- revise sentences to eliminate general introductory phrases
- revise sentences to replace abstract nouns with more concrete words.

CHOOSING ACTIVE OR PASSIVE SENTENCES

Below are three sentences; each contains exactly the same information. Read the sentences and then answer the three questions.

The application form is to be completed by you and returned by registered mail.

After the application form has been completed by you, it should be returned by registered mail.

Please complete the application form and return it by registered mail.

1. Which sentence is more direct in giving its information?

   _____

   _____

2. Which sentence focuses on what the reader should do?

   _____

   _____

3. Which sentence is the shortest?

   _____

   _____

The answer to all three questions is sentence three. Some of you may select the first or second sentence because you feel the third sentence is too direct and so may sound too rude. But busy readers of letters and memos at work prefer the third sentence because it tells them right away **who does what**.

Sentence three uses the active voice. The **active voice** focuses on the doer. In this case, the doer is understood as "you." The first and second sentences, on the other hand, are in the **passive voice**; they focus on the application form.

Your use of active or passive voice can also determine the **tone** of your writing. Read this letter:

Dear Ms Clarke

It has been brought to my attention that rolls of fabric sold by us last month may contain flaws.

If this is detected by your staff, notification should be made to me immediately. This fabric is held in quantity, and any rolls could be replaced at once.

An early reply would be appreciated so that stock allocations can be properly made.

Sincerely

Kevin Sawatzky

Kevin Sawatzky

How would you describe the tone of this letter? friendly? distant?
What gives this tone to the letter?
Now read this version of the previous letter. The content is unchanged.

Dear Ms Clarke

My supplier has told me that the rolls of fabric we sold you last week may contain flaws.
order

If your staff detect flaws, call me immediately. We hold large stocks of this fabric, and we can replace your rolls at once.

Please call me as soon as you know so that I can make proper stock allocations.

Sincerely

Kevin Sawatzky

Kevin Sawatzky

How would you describe the tone of this letter? friendly? distant?
What gives this tone to the letter?
The first letter is written in the passive voice, and the second letter is written in the active voice.

The second one is more personal and direct. Did you also notice the difference in the lengths of the two versions? The second one is shorter; active voice sentences are generally shorter than passive voice sentences.

You can often shorten passive sentences by omitting the doer. Consider, for example, the following passive sentence: "The budget was cut by the Board of Directors." In this passive sentence, the doer is included. If you omit the doer, the sentence would read "The budget was cut," which is still grammatically correct.

How do you know whether to write passive or active sentences?

Write an **active sentence** if you want to

> put the doer at the front of the sentence
> encourage action
> keep the sentence short and direct.

> The on-line Technical Communication course covers letters, memos, and short reports.

> Delivery drivers must report to Security.

> Keep away from the main rotor.

These active sentences work well. The passive would spoil them.

Write a **passive sentence** if

> the doer is unknown
> the doer doesn't matter
> you want to hide the doer.

> My car was stolen this morning.

> Helicopter blades are nitrogen-tested for cracks after every three hours of flying.

> A decision was made to dismiss three staff members.

These passive sentences work well. The active voice would spoil them.

Notice how the passive is used to focus on what's done rather than who does it: "Helicopter blades are nitrogen tested…." You will often use the passive voice in your lab write-ups when **what's done** is more important than **who does it**.

At work, the passive is sometimes used to soften bad news, "The application for a cutting permit cannot be approved," rather than the blunt active, "I am not approving your cutting permit application."

However, in general, in business and technical writing, you will want to focus on the doer, and to keep your sentences short and direct. Thus, you will usually write in the active voice.

 GUIDELINE 8:

In general, use active sentences for business and technical writing.

Rules for Arranging Active and Passive Sentences

Active

- Arrange the parts of a sentence so they describe who (or what)…does or did…what.
  Our instructor distributed copies of next week's assignment.
- Start your sentence with *I* if you are the doer.
  I need your approval to take this course.

- Use the command form of the verb if the reader is the doer.
  Submit your homework at the beginning of the class.

Passive

- Arrange the parts of a sentence so they describe what…is or was done.
  A decision was made to cut this year's budget.
- Use *by* to indicate **who** or **what** carried out the action:
  The drive chain was oiled regularly **by** the mechanic.
  The woodchipper blade was damaged **by** a stray piece of metal.
- Use *by* to indicate what method or process was used to carry out the action:
  Fuel consumption was improved **by** increasing the tire pressure.
- Use *with* to indicate what tool or instrument was used to carry out the action.
  The wheel nuts can only be loosened **with** a lug nut wrench.
  The tire pressure had been checked **with** an analog gauge.

Just like sentences in the active voice, sentences in the passive voice come in different tenses. Here is a table that allows you to compare active and passive sentences in several different tenses:

TABLE 2.1
Active and passive sentences in different tenses

Tense	Active Sentence	Passive Sentence
Present	The superintendent hires her.	She is hired.
Present progressive	The superintendent is hiring her.	She is being hired.
Future	The superintendent will hire her.	She will be hired.
Future progressive	The superintendent will be hiring her.	—
Future perfect	The superintendent will have hired her.	She will have been hired.
Present perfect	The superintendent has hired her.	She has been hired.
Past	The superintendent hired her.	She was hired.
Past progressive	The superintendent was hiring her.	She was being hired.
Past perfect	The superintendent had hired her.	She had been hired.

In addition, you may also use such words as "would," "must," and "should" in passive sentences. Here are some examples:

She **should** have been hired, but the interviewers didn't read her application thoroughly.

She **would** have been hired if they had read her entire application.

She **must** have been hired because she had all the qualifications for the job.

Practice

Read each of the following sentences. Show whether the sentence is active or passive by writing *A* or *P* beside each sentence.

1. A final check of the restaurant's kitchen was performed by the health inspector.
2. A cheque for $20,000 has been issued to Midland Equipment.
3. Complete three copies of this form and return it by first-class mail.
4. It has been decided that, effective immediately, the doors to the plant will be locked at 9 p.m. each day.
5. Approval to hire a subcontractor must be obtained from the general manager.
6. Omit unnecessary words.
7. Use of the passive voice should be avoided in business and technical writing.
8. Soo Ng represented us at last week's luncheon meeting.
9. Our house was broken into while we were on vacation.
10. A budget increase of $50,000 has been proposed by the district manager.

Practice

Rewrite each passive sentence you found in the above exercise to make it active. In some cases, you may have to add information, but do not change the meanings of the sentences.

Which of the passive sentences definitely does not need to be improved by being changed to active? Why?

GETTING TO THE POINT IN A SENTENCE

Below are four sentences taken from an article in a newspaper. I have numbered each of the sentences. See how quickly you can answer the four questions on the four sentences. For this practice, read each question *before* you look at any sentences.

Four Questions

1. Quickly, which sentence is about the first slide?

   SENTENCE NUMBER _____

2. Quickly, which sentence is about the road between Lillooet and Pemberton?

   SENTENCE NUMBER _____

3. Quickly, which sentence is about the railway passengers?

   SENTENCE NUMBER _____

4. Quickly, which sentence is about the southbound freight train?

SENTENCE NUMBER _____

Four Sentences

1. The road between Lillooet and Pemberton is down to one lane but BC Rail is back on track after heavy rain triggered weekend mudslides that shut down its line.
2. The first slide at 9 a.m. Saturday covered a 50-metre stretch of the rail line about 7 kilometres south of Lillooet in a 5-metre pile of mud and rubble.
3. Two cars of a southbound freight train were derailed by a second mudslide as the train sat waiting for the first slide to be cleared.
4. About two hundred BC Rail passengers were bused north and south around the debris on Saturday and Sunday to their destinations in North Vancouver, Lillooet, 100 Mile House, Williams Lake, Quesnel, and Prince George.

You were probably able to answer all the questions in fewer than thirty seconds. You were able to answer so quickly *because you only had to see the first few words of each sentence to know what the sentence was about.*

You've already learned to put your main idea—your purpose—at the beginning of your letters and memos. Now, do the same for your *sentences.*

GUIDELINE 9:

Show your reader what your sentence is about right away, in the first few words.

Be specific when you tell your reader what your sentence is about. Name things your reader can see, smell, hear, taste, or touch. Don't use abstractions. Don't begin your sentences with "there is/are" and "there was/were." Don't use general introductory phrases that could begin any sentences, such as "It is significant that…."

Practice

Rewrite these five sentences by putting the main idea first in each sentence. Find the main idea for each sentence by asking yourself, "What is this sentence about?"

1. There is a need for a new, faster fax machine for our office.

_____

_____

2. There is an informative catalogue available from the Purchasing Department on the latest fax machines.

_____

_____

3. The problem with buying a new fax machine outright is that it costs so much.

_____

_____

4. I found that a newer-model fax machine can be leased instead of purchased.

_____

_____

5. A point I want to emphasize here is that employees should not be allowed to use the fax machine to conduct personal business.

_____

_____

SETTING THE RIGHT TONE: BEING DIRECT *AND* POLITE

You've been learning to use the active voice and to get to the point in your sentences. However, using the active voice does not mean ordering people around, and getting to the point does not mean being rude and abrupt.

Compare these three statements made in a classroom by a student who wanted her instructor's help:

Come over here and help me.

Would you please help me when you get a chance?

I've spent a lot of time working on this software, and I've had a lot of problems with it.

Which statement is most likely to lead to the instructor's coming over to help the student? Which statement strikes you as rude? Which statement is so indirect that the instructor may not realize that the student is requesting her help?

Can you imagine a situation in which a student might order his or her instructor to do something? How about a situation in which a ceiling panel is about to fall and the student needs to tell the instructor to get out of the way?

In deciding whether a statement is appropriate or not, you need to take into account the relationship of the speaker to the listener, the situation in which they find themselves, and the purpose of the statement. The first statement, for example—"Come over here and help me"—is inappropriate because

- the instructor is in a supervisory relationship to the student
- the student's purpose is for the instructor to help her, and if she offends the instructor, the instructor is apt to find an excuse not to help her
- the situation is not an emergency.

In the contemporary workplace, you are expected to respect everyone equally, whether the person is below you, equal to you, or above you in status. For this reason, you generally do not give commands except in an emergency or when giving instructions, for example, on how to operate a piece of equipment. Nonetheless, people are generally less direct with those of higher status than with those of lower status.

The second statement—"Would you please help me when you get a chance?"—sounds less direct than the first because it

- uses the politeness form "would you" as well as the simple "please"
- acknowledges the needs and independence of the other person. "When you get a chance" shows that the student knows that the instructor is busy and that the timing of the instructor's help is up to the instructor, not the student.

The third statement—"I've spent a lot of time working on this software, and I've had a lot of problems with it"—is so indirect the instructor may not even understand that the student is requesting help. This statement poses an additional problem: in a culture as direct as Canadian business culture, such indirectness is apt to be interpreted as a waste of time and even as devious and manipulative.

People from cultures that are less direct than Canadian business culture are apt to err either by being too indirect or by overcompensating and being too direct. How can you learn the appropriate degree of directness to use when you write? Take into account the relationship between you and your reader, your purpose in writing, and the situation. Paying close attention to models of good writing, such as the model documents in this textbook, will also help.

GUIDELINE 10:

State your main idea directly, but take into account your relationship to your reader, your purpose, and your situation. Use a diplomatic supporting phrase or sentence when you feel the main idea alone would be too abrupt.

Practice

For each situation, decide which set of opening main idea statements is too direct, appropriately direct, or not direct enough.

Situation 1: You are an assistant accountant. Your computer has crashed, and you've lost data. The accountant tells you to send a message to computer resources to ask them to fix it.

Would you please fix my computer. It has crashed, and I've lost all my data.

Your department has an excellent reputation for repairing computers, such as mine, when they crash and data is lost.

Fix my computer by tomorrow morning. It has crashed, and important data has been lost.

Situation 2: You have received a scholarship from a large corporation, and you write the president of the corporation to thank her.

Your corporation performs a valuable service to the community by granting scholarships to deserving students to enable them to continue their post-secondary educations.

Thanks for the scholarship. I really wanted the money to pay my tuition.

Thank you very much for the scholarship. Without your help, I would not have been able to enroll in the nuclear medicine program at Millennium College.

Situation 3: You are the supervisor for a chemical laboratory. You've noticed that some staff are not wearing their safety goggles. You write them a reminder.

Please wear your safety goggles in the laboratory. Workers' Compensation Board regulations require you to wear them, and your own safety and that of your coworkers depend upon it.

It is important that lab staff be properly protected while working in the laboratory. Lab coats and safety goggles protect lab workers from spills.

All staff must wear safety goggles in the lab at all times.

REVIEW QUESTIONS

In your own words, answer the following questions.

1. Why are active sentences often preferred for business and technical writing?

_____

_____

_____

_____

_____

_____

_____

2. When would you use passive sentences?

_____

_____

_____

_____

_____

_____

_____

_____

3. Why should you put the main idea first in a sentence?

_____

_____

_____

_____

_____

_____

_____

_____

QUESTION SHEET

List any questions you have about this chapter:

Questions

_____
_____
_____
_____
_____
_____
_____
_____
_____
_____
_____
_____

Answers

_____
_____
_____
_____
_____
_____
_____
_____
_____
_____
_____
_____

EXERCISES

Exercise 1: Getting to the Point: Rewriting Sentences

Rewrite these sentences to make them more concise and clear. Put the main idea at the beginning of the sentence. Use active sentences, where appropriate.

1. I would like to inform you that the Polyani College of Technology and Trades will accept applications for the fall session starting next week.

   _____

   _____

2. It would be appreciated if you could send me a copy of the Polyani calendar.

   _____

   _____

3. The information that this report is based upon is my experience as a fruit picker in the Niagara region.

   _____

   _____

4. There is a course called Effective Presentations that will prepare me for my new position.

   I can do - - -

   _____

   _____

5. What I would like to do to improve my writing skills is to learn to write clear and concise sentences.

   _____

   _____

6. The skills I will need in the future will be to be able to write clearly and concisely, as I plan to enter the real estate market upon graduation.

   _____

   _____

7. I'd like to ask you to find out who is responsible for the error.

   _____

   _____

8. There is now available in the Safety and Security Office a computerized data base to help match up potential partners for car pooling.

   _____

   _____

9. The way to increase productivity and save money is to boost employee morale.

_____

_____

10. It is important that each PC user on campus take action to prevent the use of illegally copied software.

_____

_____

Exercise 2: Getting to the Point: Rewriting a Memo

The Carpool Memo

Gordon Slaney is head of Security for a medium-sized firm specializing in computerized mapping; his responsibilities include parking. Since he started bicycling to work a few months ago, Gordon has noticed that most of the vehicles in early-morning traffic jams have only one occupant—the driver. He knew he would never be able to convince everyone to cycle to work, so he volunteered to set up a car-pool program for the office. He's done some of the initial planning; now he's decided to write a memo asking the three division heads for some information and explaining why he is setting up a trial program. He knows the division heads are busy people, so he wants the memo to be clear and concise.

Help Gordon improve his memo. Put the main idea first for each sentence. Use active sentences where appropriate.

You do not need to change the order of the sentences or paragraphs.

TO: Division Heads

FROM: Gordon Slaney, Security

DATE: October 16, 199–

SUBJECT: PARTICIPANTS NEEDED FOR CAR POOL

It is necessary that we find out the number of people in your division who would like to participate in a trial car-pool program.

The feasibility of starting up a car pool was investigated by myself and the general manager. As you already know, a questionnaire was distributed to all staff to determine how many people were interested in car-pooling. It was found that almost 83 percent of our staff members support setting up a car pool.

It was felt by most respondents that we should first start the car-pool program on a four-week trial basis.

I'd like to ask you to find out how many people in your division want to sign up for the trial period. There is also the question of vehicle size; we need to know the maximum capacity of each person's car.

It would be appreciated if you would circulate the attached sign-up sheet in your division, and return it to me by the end of next week.

G. S.

Exercise 3: Getting to the Point: Rewriting a Memo

The No Food or Drinks Memo

Susan French is office manager for a small export firm. She has recently bought new, faster, more expensive computers for the office. Having noticed that some staff are drinking coffee and eating food at their computer terminals, Susan decided to write a memo asking them to stop. Her rough draft looks pretty good to her, but she's worried some of her sentences are so long her staff won't get the message.

Help Susan improve her memo. Put the main idea first for each sentence.

Memorandum

TO: All Staff

FROM: Susan French, Manager

DATE: September 13, 199—

SUBJECT: NO FOOD OR DRINKS NEAR THE COMPUTERS!

It would be appreciated if you would please not eat or drink near your computer terminal. Use the staff lounge for drinks and snacks.

A possible problem that could be caused by just one cup of coffee in the lab is that the coffee could spill on the keyboard. It could cause irreparable damage to the keyboard. It is important that it also be noted that it costs $250 to replace a keyboard. It should further be noted that damage as a result of a spill would not be covered under warranty.

I shouldn't have to remind you about the possibility of sticky keys as a result of crumbs and food spills. As you are well aware, computer keyboards have to be cleaned professionally when they are dirty, and that is expensive.

If you should happen to see co-workers with food or drink near the computers, you should not hesitate to remind them of the rules.

S. F.

Exercise 4: Getting to the Point: Rewriting a Flyer

The Green Car Flyer

Terry, who manages a car dealership in town, wants to make sure the environmental movement doesn't keep people from buying cars. He's been noticing the line of "green" products at the supermarket. People seem to like to buy green products because they are recyclable. Terry decides to prepare a flyer for potential customers reassuring them that cars are recyclable too.

Terry's prepared this rough draft of the flyer. Do you think his customers will get the message? Help Terry by **putting the main idea first in his sentences**.

GREEN CARS FOR SALE AT TERRY'S AUTO!

Buy Your Recyclable Cars Here!

Have you ever thought of buying a green car? Help the environment. Buy one of Terry's recyclable cars.

While our cars are not 100 percent recyclable, there are many parts in our cars that can be recycled.

- Approximately 70 percent of any car on our lot is made of metal. It is possible to melt down our car body and use the steel to produce new steel—not to mention the aluminum engine block that can also be recycled.

- You can be sure that 12 percent of any car on our lot is plastic. We now know that some plastics can be melted down and used as fillers for new plastics.

- Any car on our lot is made up of 6 percent fluids. Among these fluids are included used engine oils, which can be reprocessed into lubricating oils. It should also be mentioned that coolants (antifreeze) can also be recycled and reused.

- Rubber constitutes 4 percent of any car on our lot. It is quite easy to recycle rubber tires and turn them into such items as rubber mats and mudguards.

- Our lot has cars that are 3 percent glass. It is often possible to salvage and resell this glass.

- Included in the final 5 percent of the car is the battery, which you should be advised can also be recycled.

For a car that is nearly 100 percent recyclable, hurry over to Terry's. We don't expect our green cars to last!

Exercise 5: Using the Active Voice

The Computer Virus Memo

Maria Fernandez is systems manager at a large accounting firm. Recently, staff have been complaining about the number of computer viruses that are slowing down or destroying their work. A computer virus attack can destroy years of work in seconds; Maria is worried that one day some valuable data may be lost.

Maria decided to write a brief memo telling everyone what to do if a virus attacks a computer. She's included all the necessary details, but she's worried staff won't get the message because some of the sentences don't focus on **what the reader should do.**

Help Maria improve the memo. Change passive voice sentences to active voice. Following Maria's memo is some background information on computer viruses.

TO: All Staff

FROM: Maria Fernandez, Systems Manager

DATE: November 19, 199—

SUBJECT: WHAT TO DO IF A VIRUS ATTACKS YOUR COMPUTER

These steps should be followed as soon as you realize a computer virus is attacking your computer:

1. The power should be turned off immediately.

2. The computer should then be turned on again using a "write-protect" copy of your system diskette.

3. An anti-viral program should be used to check every file on your hard disk.

4. Your back-up files should then be used to restore all your data to your hard disk.

5. Finally, all of your floppy disks should be checked to make sure you find any viruses.

This memo should be posted near your computer. Please call me if you have any questions about computer viruses.

M. F.

WHAT IS A COMPUTER VIRUS?

A computer virus is a computer program that is written as a joke or a prank; or it can also be written to destroy information. A virus will attack the hard disk on your computer, destroying years of information in a few minutes. A virus can erase, lose, or hide information on your computer.

Here are explanations of some of the terms used in the memo:

Write-Protect File: *Write-protect* means no information can be written on to the diskette. Therefore, viruses cannot attack this diskette.

Anti-Viral Program: An *anti-viral program* is a computer program designed to find viruses on your hard disk.

Exercise 6: Using the Passive Voice

THE PHYSICS LAB WRITE-UP

You will often use the passive in lab write-ups. This is because *what's done* is more important than *who does it.* The results of your experiment should be the same regardless of who is performing it.

The following steps are taken from an experiment performed by students in their physics lab. Change the steps from the active to the passive in the procedure section of the lab write-up.

Included are a sketch and a list of the apparatus to help you understand what the students performing the experiment did.

APPARATUS

- spring constant apparatus, which includes a metre stick and an L-shaped stand
- metal position guide
- coil spring
- set of weights from 0.200 to 1.000 kg
- stopwatch

Figure 2–1

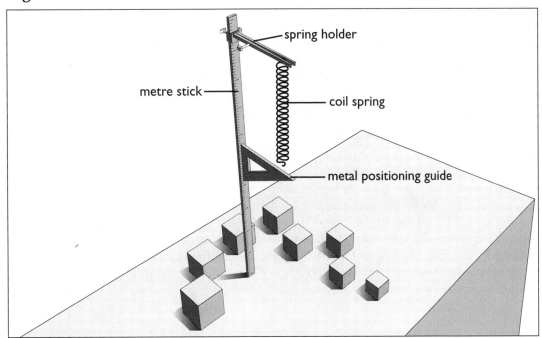

The following steps are in the active because they are instructions for the experiment. Each step is a command that tells the reader what to do. For the procedure section of the report, the writer wants to record what was done. Rewrite these steps in the passive, in the past tense, for the procedure section of the lab write-up.

STEPS

1. Suspend the coil spring from the spring holder:
    1.1 Loosen the wing nut on the spring holder to separate the two pieces of metal.
    1.2 Place the end of the spring in the middle of this gap.
    1.3 Tighten the wing nut to close the gap.
2. Set the top of the coil spring at the 0 position on the metre stick:
    2.1 Loosen the wing nut that keeps the spring holder in place on the metre stick.
    2.2 Slide the spring holder up or down until the top of the spring is at the 0 position on the metre stick.
    2.3 Tighten the wing nut to keep the spring holder in place on the metre stick.
3. Measure the length of the coil spring:
    3.1 Use your thumb to hold the metal position guide in place on the metre stick.
    3.2 To obtain an accurate measurement, slide the metal position guide up or down with your thumb until you've lined up the bottom of the spring with the metre stick.
    3.3 Sighting along the metal position guide, read the measurement on the metre stick that lines up with the bottom of the coil spring.
4. Gently hang a 0.200 kg mass on the end of the coil spring.
5. Measure the length of the coil spring bearing the 0.200 kg mass using the metal position guide to line up the bottom of the spring with the metre stick.
6. With your hand pull the 0.200 kg mass down 5 cm.
7. Release the 0.200 kg mass.
8. Using the stopwatch, measure the time for the 0.200 kg mass to make 50 complete oscillations.
9. Remove the 0.200 kg mass from the end of the coil spring.
10. Repeat steps 4 through 9 for masses 0.300 kg, 0.400 kg, 0.500 kg, 0.600 kg, 0.700 kg, 0.800 kg and 1.0 kg.

Exercise 7: Using the Active Voice

REPORTS ON TWO LAB ACCIDENTS

This exercise contains reports of two accidents that actually happened. The first accident took place in a chemistry lab. The second accident took place in a physics lab. The students involved were asked to hand in written reports on the accidents.

The students wrote their reports as they would lab write-ups. They used the passive to carefully hide the names of the doers! However, in the case of an accident, the name of the doer is important. Lab instructors need to know the identity of the doer in case someone was hurt or in case the instructors need to find out more information about the accident.

Rewrite the students' reports by changing the sentences from passive to active, and providing names wherever needed.

THE CHEMISTRY LAB

Dirt was being measured and weighed for a bacteria experiment. The dirt was being placed into a pan when the beaker was knocked on to the floor by my elbow. No injury was sustained by me. The dirt was swept up and the glass placed in the garbage can, which is for glass only.

THE PHYSICS LAB

The experiment being performed was the thermistor lab on converting resistance to temperature. The thermometer was being shaken while being moved around the room as I walked to the back of the lab to get my lab book, which had found its way to another student's lab table. Attention was not being paid to the shaking of the thermometer because of the concentration on obtaining the lab book. The thermometer was dropped on the floor. The capillary tube was shattered. Little droplets of mercury could be seen on the floor. A lab technician was notified. As instructed by the lab technician, I made sure the mercury was cleaned up with a special brush and broom that is only used for mercury clean-up by me.

chapter three

COMBINING YOUR SENTENCES TO SHOW THE RELATIONSHIP BETWEEN YOUR IDEAS

Combining sentences will help you write more efficiently by enabling you to communicate more than one idea in one sentence. By choosing the right linking word to combine your sentences, you will also save your reader time because your reader will only have to read your sentence once to see how your ideas are related.

In Chapter 1, you learned that if you don't know the purpose of your writing, your reader won't either. In Chapter 2, you discovered that writing straightforward sentences requires straightforward thinking and good judgment. In this chapter, you will become even more aware of the connection between writing and thinking as you are challenged to choose the linking word that communicates precisely the logical connection between your ideas.

Communication Outcomes

When you finish this chapter, you will be able to

- explain why you sometimes need to combine sentences in your writing
- combine sentences when you want to show that the ideas in a sentence are equally important
- combine sentences when you want to show that one idea in a sentence is more important than another.

Language Outcomes

When you finish this chapter, you will be able to

- choose an appropriate **coordinating conjunction** or **conjunctive adverb** to logically connect ideas that are equally important
- use commas correctly when you use a coordinating conjunction to join sentences
- use a semicolon and a comma when you join sentences with a conjunctive adverb
- identify and eliminate repeated subjects and verbs to join sentences, where appropriate
- choose an appropriate **subordinating conjunction** to logically connect ideas when one idea is more important than another
- change a sentence to a phrase
- use commas correctly when you use a subordinating conjunction to join sentences
- identify and correct comma splices
- identify and correct run-on sentences.

COMBINING SENTENCES

Why Combine Sentences?

1. Combining simple sentences will help you **show the relationship between ideas** in a sentence. Look at the following two simple sentences:

   This software package is the least expensive.

   It doesn't have all the functions we need.

   Is the package recommended *because* it's the least expensive? Is the package recommended *although* it doesn't have all the functions? Someone reading these two simple sentences won't know the answer to these questions. However, if you join these two sentences, using *although*, the relationship between the two ideas is clearer.

   Although this software package is the least expensive, it doesn't have all the functions we need.

2. Combining simple sentences will also **add variety to your writing**; your sentences will be more interesting to read. Read the following simple sentences:

   Our office decided to buy a new, faster computer system.

   We wanted to make the business more productive.

We wanted to make the business more efficient.

We hired a consultant.

The consultant's job was to recommend a system we should buy.

You could make this material more interesting by combining sentences:

Because we wanted to make the business more productive and efficient, our office decided to buy a new, faster computer system. We hired a consultant to recommend a system we should buy.

GUIDELINE 11:

Combine sentences to show the relationship between your ideas and to add variety to your writing.

In this section, you will learn how to combine sentences to show when ideas are equally important, and to emphasize one idea over another.

COMBINING SENTENCES TO GIVE EQUAL EMPHASIS TO IDEAS

You can combine two different but equally important ideas in several ways:

- Use a comma and a coordinating conjunction.
- Eliminate repeated subjects and verbs.
- Use a semicolon and a conjunctive adverb.

Use a Comma and a Coordinating Conjunction

You can show *how* the ideas in two sentences are related by using a comma and one of the following linking words. These linking words are called **coordinating conjunctions.**

- and
- but
- for
- or
- nor
- so (not "so that")
- yet.

  Joining two sentences with one of these linking words tells your reader that each idea is equally important. When you use these linking words to join complete sentences, follow this pattern:

Complete sentence, AND complete sentence.

Complete sentence, BUT complete sentence.

Complete sentence, OR complete sentence.

Complete sentence, FOR complete sentence.

Complete sentence, YET complete sentence.

Complete sentence, SO complete sentence.

Complete sentence, NOR complete sentence.

Punctuation Rules for Coordinating Conjunctions

1. You must have a complete sentence on each side of the linking word.
2. Use a *comma* before the linking word.

The following pairs of ideas could be effectively combined by the linking words *and, but,* or *or*:

I bought an old van. I towed it home.

The new wage structure was announced this week. It won't take effect until October.

We could meet her at the airport. We could meet her at the factory.

Now read the combined sentences:

I bought an old van, **and** I towed it home.

The new wage structure was announced this week, **but** it won't take effect until October.

We could meet her at the airport, **or** we could meet her at the factory.

Choosing a Linking Word

Choose an appropriate linking word to join your sentences—one that shows the relationship between the sentences you're joining.

For example, you should not always use the linking word *and* to join sentences. Table 3.1 gives the meanings of the seven coordinating conjunctions.

Use Table 3.1 to help you choose linking words that logically connect the ideas in your sentences.

TABLE 3.1
Linking words: coordinating conjunctions

Word	Meaning
and	shows addition of ideas *Fumi works full-time at a bakery, and he takes evening courses two nights a week.*
but	shows contrast *I wanted to start my program in September, but I had to take a physics course first.*
for	shows reason and support *I like to study in the library on Friday nights, for it's usually very quiet.*
or	shows alternative idea *I must finish this assignment tonight, or I'll have to hand it in late.*
yet	shows contrast *I've read that assignment three times, yet I still don't understand the main idea.*
nor	shows negative alternative *I don't want to take an extra evening course, nor do I want to go to school in the summer.*
so	shows result or consequence *I hadn't read the assignment, so I couldn't participate in the group discussion.*

Practice

Use a comma and a logical joining word to combine the following pairs of sentences. Study the table on the previous page if you are not sure about the meaning of some of the joining words.

1. We sell fir to the United States. We sell red cedar to Japan.

   _____

   _____

   _____

2. Canadian trade with Japan is expected to reach $40 billion by the year 2000. Trade with South Korea, Singapore, Hong Kong, and Taiwan will top $10 billion.

   _____

   _____

   _____

3. There could be an ignition problem. There could be a fuel blockage.

   _____

   _____

   _____

4. You should pay your fees. The college opens on September 6.

   _____

   _____

   _____

Using a linking word and a comma is one way to join simple sentences. Here is another way:

Eliminate Repeated Subjects and Verbs

You can sometimes make *and/but/or* sentences shorter if

- the second half has the **same subject** as the first
                          OR
- the second half has the **same subject and verb** as the first half.

EXAMPLE ONE:

I bought an old van, and I towed it home.

Both parts of this sentence have the same subject, so you can drop the second *I* and you can drop the comma.

I bought an old van and towed it home.

EXAMPLE TWO:

My ticket was delivered, but it was not delivered in time.

The second part of the sentence has the same subject and verb as the first part, so you can drop the *it* and *was delivered* from the second part. You can also omit the comma.

My ticket was delivered but not in time.

Rules for Eliminating Repeated Subjects and Verbs

1. You can eliminate repeated subjects and verbs in *and/but/or* sentences if the second half of the sentence has either the same subject or the same subject and verb as the first half.

2. Drop the comma when you omit either a repeated subject or a repeated subject and verb.

Here is a third way to join sentences to show that ideas have equal importance.

Use a Semicolon and a Conjunctive Adverb

A semicolon (;) is sometimes used with a linking word or expression to join two complete thoughts. These words and phrases show specific relationships between clauses, so it's important to think about the meaning of the sentences you're combining when you choose one of these linking words. Here is a list of common linking words and phrases with their meanings.

TABLE 3.2
Linking words and phrases: conjunctive adverbs

Your Purpose	Word/Phrase You Should Use
To add an idea:	in addition, furthermore, also
To show time or sequence:	meanwhile, first, second, then, next, later, finally
To contrast:	however, nevertheless, though, in contrast, on the other hand
To show result:	therefore, thus, consequently, as a result
To emphasize:	in fact, of course, indeed, certainly
To provide an example:	for example, for instance
To generalize or summarize:	in general, overall, in short

Punctuation Rule for Using Linking Words/Expressions

When you use a conjunctive adverb as a linking word, use a semicolon (;) before the linking word and a comma after the linking word.

> He doubted that the new diet plan would work; however, he decided to try it.

You already know how to join sentences to show that ideas are of equal importance. For example, you can use a linking word (and, but, for) and a comma.

You should, however, avoid *overusing* linking words such as *and, but, for, so, however, therefore,* or any of the linking words listed in the tables of coordinating and conjunctive adverbs. Used some of the time, these words add variety to your writing. If you overuse these words, your sentences will look like you've simply strung together several ideas; your sentences will lack emphasis.

COMBINING SENTENCES TO EMPHASIZE ONE IDEA OVER ANOTHER

Read the following sentences:

> I want to study electronics full-time in September, so I am enrolling in a pre-entry program in January, and that way I can finish all the prerequisites for electronics.

> Because I want to study electronics full-time in September, I am enrolling in a pre-entry program in January to finish all the prerequisites.

Which sentence is the more effective? Why? Which sentence more clearly shows the relationship between ideas?

The second sentence is the more effective. Here the writer has used the linking word *because* to emphasize the relationship between ideas in the sentence. In the second sentence, "because" tells the reader that the idea *Because I want to study electronics full-time in September* is less important than *I am enrolling in a pre-entry program in January to finish all the prerequisites.*

In this section, you will learn two ways to join sentences, so that one idea is less important than another:

- Make one sentence less important than another by adding a subordinating conjunction.
- Turn the less important sentence into a phrase.

Use a Subordinating Conjunction

When you want to give equal emphasis to two or more ideas, you join them by using the linking words *and, but, for, or, nor, so, yet.*

If you want to show that one idea is less important than another, you need to use linking words such as *although, if, when, because,* and *after.* Grammar textbooks call these subordinating conjunctions. Table 3.3 gives a list of subordinating words with their meanings. Look at the following example, where two sentences have been joined using the linking word *after:*

> After I had finished my final exam, I went home and slept for two days.

The linking word *after* shows the relationship between the two parts of the sentence. The idea that the writer wants to emphasize is expressed as a complete thought: *I went home and slept for two days.* The less important idea starts with the linking word: *After I had finished my final exam.*

Notice that the idea *After I had finished my final exam* doesn't make sense by itself; it has to be joined to the rest of the sentence.

TABLE 3.3
Linking words: subordinating conjunctions

Your Purpose	Words You Should Use
To show a relationship of time or sequence:	before, after, ever since, since, as long as, while, until, when
To show a relationship of purpose or result:	so that, in order that, that
To show contrast or concession:	although, if, even though, though, while
To show a relationship of cause or reason:	as, as if, as though, whereas, because
To show a relationship of place:	where, wherever
To show a relationship of condition:	if, unless, whether or not

Change a Sentence to a Phrase

If you want to join two simple sentences, but you want to emphasize only one idea, keep the most important idea as a complete sentence and make the less important idea a phrase. Read the following sentences; then look at how they have been joined. The phrase is in *italics*.

Gerald Drake is our accounts manager.

He has been with the company for more than five years.

Gerald Drake, *our accounts manager*, has been with the company for more than five years.

Rules for Punctuating Sentences Joined with Linking Words

1. Don't use a comma when you use a subordinating conjunction as a linking word *between* two ideas:

   The noise level exceeded 90dB **because** the ventilators were at full power.

   You probably use an electric block heater to prevent your vehicle's engine from freezing **if** you live in a cold region of Canada.

2. Sometimes the new sentence is stronger if you place the linking word at the *beginning*. Doing this produces a natural pause between the ideas, and you should then use a comma before the second idea.

   Because the ventilators were at full power, the noise level exceeded 90 dB.

   If you live in a cold region of Canada, you probably use an electric block heater to prevent your vehicle's engine from freezing.

AVOIDING SENTENCE ERRORS

If you follow the conventions in this unit and use common sense, you will avoid two common errors in sentence construction. They are

- the comma splice
- the run-on sentence.

The following two sentences have those respective errors. The sentences happen to be grammatically wrong, and as a result *they don't make sense*.

The drill is the cheapest, it's the best one.

The fan was turned down it became noisy.

Is the drill recommended because it's cheap? Would you trust this statement or its writer?

Did the fan become noisy as soon as it was turned down? Was it turned down after it had become noisy? Would you trust the writer to write maintenance reports?

Here are the sentences rewritten. Their ideas are combined correctly, and the sentences now make sense.

Although this drill is the cheapest, it's the best one.

When the fan was turned down, it became noisy.

Practice

Combine these pairs of simple sentences. Use any suitable linking word, but do not use a comma.

1. A thunderstorm arrived over downtown. Many car alarms came on.

   _____

   _____

2. Skydiving seems dangerous. It's more popular each year.

   _____

   _____

3. The shipment arrived. I checked the invoice.

   _____

   _____

Combine these pairs of simple sentences using any suitable linking word. Omit repeated words.

1. You are looking for an energy-efficient house. Consider the R-2000 house.

   _____

   _____

   _____

2. R-2000 homes were developed in the 1980s. R-2000 homes still exceed building code requirements for insulation.

    _____

    _____

    _____

3. They are designed to save energy costs. They are not designed to save building costs.

    _____

    _____

    _____

REVIEW QUESTIONS

In your own words, answer the following questions.

1. What are two reasons for combining sentences?

    _____

    _____

2. Use your own words to define

    COMMA SPLICE:_____

    RUN-ON SENTENCE: _____

QUESTION SHEET

List any questions you have about this unit:

Questions

_____

_____

_____

_____

_____

_____

_____

_____

_____

_____

_____

Answers

_____

_____

_____

_____

_____

_____

_____

_____

_____

_____

_____

_____

◢ EXERCISES

Exercise 1: Combining Sentences

Below are numbered groups of sentences. Combine the sentences in each group into one sentence. Omit repeated words, but do not change the meanings of the sentences.

Reducing Your Household Garbage

1. Many things around your house can be saved. *as*
   Many things around your house can be reused.

   _____

   _____

   _____

2. You can give magazines and books to friends. *or*
   You can donate magazines and books to hospitals. *or*
   You can sell them to used bookstores.

   _____

   _____

   _____

3. You may want to just throw them away. ②
   ① You can donate old clothes and appliances to charitable organizations. *or*

   _____

   _____

   _____

4. *thought*
   We usually buy too much food,
   Twenty percent of all the food we buy ends up in the garbage.

   _____

   _____

   _____

5. Keep track of the food you have on hand.
   You can use groceries while they are still fresh. *by*

   _____

   _____

   _____

Recycling Newspapers

6. Most people think about recycling.
   They think about old newspapers.

   _____

   _____

   _____

7. Newspapers have been the major component of recycling programs for many years.
   Newspapers make up 10 percent of total residential waste.

   _____

   _____

   _____

8. Old newspapers can be de-inked at a chemical plant.
   They can then be processed to make fresh newsprint.
   Newsprint is the paper on which newspapers are printed.

   _____

   _____

   _____

9. Most old newspaper is shipped to the Far East for processing.
   Some old newspaper is shipped to a plant in the United States.

   _____

   _____

   _____

10. Old newspapers are processed to make boxboard.
    Boxboard is a lightweight cardboard.
    Boxboard is used to make cereal boxes and shoe boxes.

    _____

    _____

    _____

Collecting and Recycling Paint

11. When improperly disposed of into sewers or landfills, old paint can contaminate. It can contaminate soil, water, and air.

_____

_____

_____

12. Paint manufacturers are organizing a paint collection program. The program is being paid for by the paint manufacturers.

_____

_____

_____

13. To ensure that everyone has a chance to safely dispose of old paint, you are asked to limit your returns. The limit on returns is ten 4-litre cans per person per day.

_____

_____

_____

Recycling Guidelines for Office Moves

14. The Recycling Department can provide large, black-wheeled recycling barrels. You can also put recyclable office waste in cardboard boxes. The cardboard boxes must be sealed and labelled.

_____

_____

_____

15. We cannot move overflowing boxes of paper. We cannot move overstuffed green and white recycling bags. They are too difficult to handle for custodians and recycling staff.

_____

_____

_____

Exercise 2: Combining Sentences

Below are numbered groups of sentences. Combine the sentences in each group into one sentence.

Static Electricity, Smoke and Sunlight, and Your Computers

1. We are having a problem with static electricity in our computer lab.
    I am placing all the computers on antistatic pads.

    _____

    _____

    _____

2. Computers are cooled by fans.
    Fans drag in smoke from the surrounding air.

    _____

    _____

    _____

3. The contacts on the plug-in chips become coated with tobacco tar.
    An intermittent loss of contact results.
    The computer malfunctions.

    _____

    _____

    _____

4. The computer was kept in direct sunlight.
    The structural components became warped.
    The structural components no longer fit properly.
    Rubber parts, such as belts, became stretched.

    _____

    _____

    _____

    _____

Carpal Tunnel Syndrome (CTS)

5. CTS is an occupational injury.
   CTS is brought on by repetitive work or movement.

   _____

   _____

   _____

6. CTS is a pain in the hand.
   CTS is sometimes called "writer's cramp."

   _____

   _____

   _____

7. The carpal tunnel is a passageway composed of bone and ligament.
   The major nerve system of the forearm passes throughout the carpal tunnel into the hand.

   _____

   _____

   _____

   _____

8. Repetitive motion can narrow the tunnel leading into the hand.
   The narrowed tunnel compresses the nerve.
   Pain or numbness in the hand occurs.

   _____

   _____

   _____

9. Women are more susceptible to CTS than men.
   Women tend to do the kinds of work that causes CTS.
   Women's carpal tunnel space is smaller.

   _____

   _____

   _____

10. You're working at a computer keyboard.
    Make sure your fingers are lower than your wrists.
    Don't rest the heel of your hands on the keyboard.

    _____

    _____

    _____

11. Type with a soft touch.
    Don't pound the keys.

    _____

    _____

12. You're working at a computer keyboard.
    Your hands hurt.
    Stop working.

    _____

    _____

Eye Strain and Muscle Fatigue

13. Look up from your work.
    Focus on something in the distance for a few seconds.
    These short vision breaks reduce eye strain.

    _____

    _____

    _____

14. Prop your elbows on the table.
    Cover your eyes with your hands.
    Imagine you are sitting in the sun on a warm summer's day.
    Imagine you are looking out at a calm sea.

    _____

    _____

    _____

15. Children are told to sit still.
    Children are told not to squirm in their seats.
    Squirming helps prevent muscle fatigue for both children and adults.

    _____

    _____

    _____

16. The force on your spinal column when you are standing is less than 325 newtons per square centimetre.
The force on your spinal column when you are sitting is 450 newtons per square centimetre.

_____

_____

_____

17. You're working at the computer.
Rest your feet firmly on the floor.
Your thighs should be parallel to the floor.

_____

_____

_____

18. Your weight should be evenly distributed on your hips.
Remove your wallet from your back pocket.
A fat wallet will cause you to tip slightly to one side in your chair.

_____

_____

_____

19. Raise your shoulders towards your ears.
Hold your shoulders towards your ears for up to five seconds.
This will relieve tension and soreness in the shoulders and neck area.

_____

_____

_____

Physical Demands of Work

20. The amount of force your muscles and other tissues must exert to handle an object depends on many factors.
These factors include your posture, the speed of your movements, the duration of the exertion, and the weight and friction of the load you are handling.

_____

_____

_____

_____

_____

21. Both high and low friction can increase the force you must exert.
    Pushing loads on carpets requires extra force.
    Holding tools with slippery handles requires extra force.
    Gripping an object while you are wearing gloves requires extra force.

    _____

    _____

    _____

    _____

22. Gripping objects more forcefully causes fatigue.
    Gripping objects more forcefully increases the risk of injury.
    Your gloves are too big.
    Your gloves are too small.
    Your gloves are too stiff.
    Your gloves are made of a slippery material.
    The force needed to grip objects increases.

    _____

    _____

    _____

    _____

    _____

23. Non-fabric gloves are made of rubber, PVC, or neoprene.
    Non-fabric gloves can irritate your hands.
    Non-fabric gloves don't provide enough ventilation.
    Wear non-fabric gloves only when necessary.

    _____

    _____

    _____

    _____

24. You have problems sleeping at home.
    You are not as alert at work.
    You fall asleep at work.
    You have problems with your health.
    You have problems with your stomach.
    You are not adapting well to shiftwork.
    You make more mistakes at work.
    You are more apt to be injured at work.

    _____

    _____

    _____

    _____

    _____

25. Laser printers are usually quiet.
    Some dot matrix printers are quieter than others.
    A noisy printer can be moved.
    A noisy printer can be replaced.
    A noisy printer can be sound-proofed.
    Sound insulation partitions can be installed between the noisy printer and your work station.
    Noise can affect concentration.
    Noise can keep you from being able to have a normal conversation.

    _____

    _____

    _____

    _____

    _____

    _____

chapter four

WRITING IN A TECHNICAL STYLE: CHOOSING YOUR WORDS CAREFULLY

In Chapter 3, you learned how to combine sentences to show your reader how your ideas are related. In this chapter, you will learn how to choose the exact words you need to tell your reader what you mean in as few words as possible. You will know you have succeeded when your reader understands your sentences on the first reading.

To write precisely and concisely (in as few words as possible to achieve your purpose) is to write in the technical style. In this style, you, the writer, do the thinking on behalf of your reader and exercise your judgment to choose your words wisely. By doing so, you will spare your reader the time and effort of having to read your sentences more than once.

Communication Outcomes

When you have finished this chapter, you should be able to

- explain why you need to use a plain and simple style in your technical and business writing
- identify three major kinds of readability blocks
- list four ways to eliminate unnecessary words from your writing
- explain the advantage of putting you and your reader into your writing
- explain the difference between measurable and non-measurable information.

Language Outcomes

When you have finished this chapter, you should be able to

- use a plain and simple style to improve the readability of your writing
- revise sentences to put you and your reader into your writing
- revise sentences to replace or eliminate words and phrases that interfere with readability
- revise sentences to eliminate unnecessary words
- revise sentences to replace imprecise words with measurable information.

TECHNICAL STYLE

Why use straightforward language?

In Chapter 1, you learned to define the purpose of your writing by answering the question, "What do I want my reader to do?" This is because the purpose of all business and technical writing is to get your reader to do something, such as follow your instructions, buy your product, grant your request, accept your proposal, or build something the way you want it built. To achieve your purpose, you will need to talk to your reader in straightforward, plain language.

When you read your writing aloud, you will find it difficult to read any awkward phrases or overly long sentences. If your sentences are difficult for you to read, you can imagine how hard it will be for your reader.

GUIDELINE 12:

Read your writing aloud to make sure you are "talking" to your reader in a natural, straightforward style.

Awkward phrases and overly long sentences are readability blocks for your reader because they keep your reader from understanding your writing quickly and easily.

Three main readability blocks you will learn about in this chapter are (1) "big" words; (2) overused expressions and business jargon; and (3) trendy expressions and slang.

The three tables on the following pages show examples of the types of readability blocks and offer plain and simple solutions. The left column in each table, titled "Don't

Use," lists words and phrases that are frequently misused. The right column, titled "Instead Use," gives words and phrases that you *should* use.

We've presented the lists of words in tables, so that you can quickly refer to the tables when you are revising your own writing. Tables and other types of graphics are also widely used in business and technical writing. A writer of a report comparing two types of cable cutters, for example, might choose to use a table to list the main differences between the cable cutters. Presenting the information in the table allows the report readers to quickly see the differences between the two types of cable cutters. We have used tables throughout this book, so you can see some examples of how and when to use tables in your own technical and business writing.

The words and phrases listed in the "Don't Use" columns of each of the tables have not been randomly chosen. We've chosen words and phrases that are most frequently used, or misused, in both classrooms and workplaces. As you read the "Don't Use" column of each table, circle the words and phrases that you use most often, and then check the "Instead Use" column to find suitable replacement words. When you read the "Don't Use" examples, you will also see words or phrases that you have seen in e-mail, memos, letters, or reports; for example, you may have seen some of the overused expressions, such as "enclosed please find" or "please be advised that." Some of these expressions are still used in letters and memos, but their use is decreasing. Do *not* use these in your own writing.

If your first language is not English, use an English-English dictionary when you need to look up a word. If you use a bilingual dictionary, you may mistakenly choose words that are not appropriate to the situation you're writing about; for example, an English-English dictionary will tell you if a word is out of date. If a word isn't listed in your dictionary, you shouldn't use it in business or technical writing.

Your dictionary will tell you if the word is "standard" or "nonstandard"; use only standard words in business and technical writing. The notation *sl.* or *slang*, for example, will appear after a word if it is slang. Many people use slang when they are talking to friends, but it is inappropriate for professional communication.

GUIDELINE 13:

Use an English-English dictionary to make sure that the words you use are standard and appropriate to the context.

Do not use words that are labelled nonstandard, informal, substandard, or dialect.

BIG WORDS

GUIDELINE 14:

Use natural, everyday words with which your reader is familiar.

Using short, familiar words will not offend your reader; pretentious and pompous words, however, may irritate your reader and will definitely make your writing difficult to understand. Here is a list of some words that block readability.

TABLE 4.1
Readability blocks: big words

Don't Use	Instead Use
advise *	tell *
approximately	about
ascertain	find out
commence	start
endeavour	try
fabricate	build, make
facilitate	help
prior to	before
proceed	go
render assistance	help
subsequent to	after
terminate	end
transmit	send
utilize	use
viable option	choice

*In some situations, you will need to use *advise*. Use advise when you mean *giving advice*.
Our staff can **advise** students on what programs to take.
Use *tell* for anything other than giving advice.
Please **tell** staff in your department that the new computers will be installed by the end of April.

OVERUSED EXPRESSIONS AND BUSINESS JARGON

GUIDELINE 15:
Do *not* use overused expressions or business jargon.

You should always delete or simplify all of the phrases and expressions in the following table; they are slow, wordy, and old-fashioned. Some of these overused expressions still appear in letters and memos, but their use is decreasing. Do *not* use these words and expressions in your writing.

TABLE 4.2
Readability blocks: overused expressions

Don't Use	Instead Use
As per your request...	delete
Attached herewith...	Attached is/here is...
Be of assistance...	help
Enclosed please find...	Enclosed is/here is...
If any questions should arise, please do not hesitate to contact the undersigned.	Please call me if you have any questions.
In reference to...	delete
It has come to my attention that...	delete
It would be appreciated if...	delete
Pending receipt of...	When we receive...
Please be advised that...	delete
Thanking you for your kind attention...	delete
This is to inform you...	delete
We beg to advise you...	delete
We kindly thank you for...	delete

TRENDY EXPRESSIONS AND SLANG

 GUIDELINE 16:

Do not use trendy expressions and slang.

Closely related to trite phrases and overused expressions are trendy words or expressions; trendy expressions soon become trite and meaningless because of overuse. They fill up space but add nothing to your writing.

The much-used expression "the bottom line," for example, is an accounting term; it means the final figure showing profit or loss. Now the expression is used to mean any final deadline or result: *The bottom line is that we have to lay off ten people.*

Another readability block is slang. Slang is too informal for business and technical communication. Like "big" words, slang can limit or even block your communication with a reader. Some examples of slang are *get on someone's case, rip off.*

Here are examples of some common trendy words and expressions that should be omitted or replaced.

TABLE 4.3
Readability blocks: trendy expressions

Don't Use	Instead Use
the bottom line	delete
cost-effective	delete
dialogue	discussion
facilitate	ease, allow, simplify, permit
hopefully	delete
impact (as a verb)	affect, increase, reduce
implement	start, carry out
liaise	meet, work with
optimum	best
parameters	factors, guidelines, variables, limitations
problematic	a problem
really cool	delete
vis-à-vis	about, of

PLAIN AND SIMPLE STYLE

As the examples on the previous pages suggest, the solution to readability blocks is to use a **plain** writing style to talk to your readers.

Look at the following examples of difficult sentences, which have been rewritten in a plain style to improve their readability.

Difficult	Approximately two hundred students utilize this computer lab every day.
Rewrite	About two hundred students use this computer lab every day.
Difficult	Please advise us of the date on which the program will commence, so we can transmit the information to you.
Rewrite	Please tell us when the program starts, so we can send you the information.
Difficult	The major causal factor of the increase in order cancellations is the new inventory system.
Rewrite	The new inventory system is the major cause of the increase in order cancellations.
Difficult	The most viable option is to terminate weekend opening hours.
Rewrite	The best choice is to close on weekends.
Difficult	By utilizing our present staff, we can save up to $10,000.
Rewrite	By using our present staff, we can save up to $10,000.

Practice

Read the difficult sentences on the next two pages. Then rewrite the sentences in a plain style to improve their readability. Be careful to try and keep the same meanings as those of the original sentences.

1. Please inform all your students that classes have been cancelled in order to facilitate increased student participation in this year's open house.

   _____

   _____

2. At my most recent place of employment, I utilized AutoCad and Excel.

   _____

   _____

3. If you have any further questions in regard to the aforementioned problems, please do not hesitate to contact the undersigned.

   _____

   _____

4. Enclosed please find the records of the unpaid loans that have accumulated over the past five years.

   _____

   _____

5. Subsequent to my interview for the position of junior software engineer, I wrote a thank-you letter to the company's human resources manager.

   _____

   _____

6. This is to inform you that your correspondence of October 16 has been received by us.

   _____

   _____

7. Prior to November 20, kindly advise us of approximately how many people will be attending the workshop, so we can arrange for refreshments and seating.

   _____

   _____

8. The vehicle operator brought the truck to a stationary position in close proximity to the ditch.

   _____

   _____

9. Please give an indication of the probable completion date for the erection of the three-way stop signs.

_____

_____

10. As per your request, here is the information regarding the proposed expansion.

_____

_____

YOU AND YOUR READER

In Chapter 2, you learned one way to include people in your writing: by using the active voice.

By using a plain and simple style, you will also involve the reader in your writing.

You'll notice that the rewritten sentences on the previous pages sound more natural—closer to the way you talk—than the original sentences. This is because using a plain style based on spoken English encourages you, the writer, to put **yourself and your reader** into your writing.

One technique to help you put yourself and your reader into your writing is to imagine a conversation between you and your reader. Another technique is to talk to a partner before you write, checking that your partner has understood your message quickly and easily.

Practice

Here is the wording of a standard company reply card. The company has obviously taken care to put itself and its readers into the document.

To appreciate how hard the writer worked, circle every personal pronoun in the reply card.

IF WE CAN'T SAVE YOU MONEY, WE DON'T DESERVE YOUR BUSINESS.

We appreciate your interest in XYZ products and services. We've enclosed the information you requested.

We welcome the opportunity to be of further assistance. To help us help you, will you please take a moment to complete the brief postage-paid form attached to this memo?

If you have an immediate need, just telephone the divisional office nearest you and ask for our chief engineer. Our office numbers are listed on the back of this card for your convenience.

Thank you.

Here are additional examples of an overly official, bureaucratic style and a plain style that involves the reader.

Bureaucratic   This is to acknowledge receipt of the "home-office" pilot project suggestion.

Plain   Thank you for sending us your "home-office" pilot project suggestion.

Bureaucratic   The public and staff are advised that all vehicles should be locked when parked on the premises.

Plain   Please remember to lock your car when you park in our lot.

Each of the rewritten examples above *involves readers* by speaking directly to them. You'll notice also that the rewritten examples are more persuasive. Readers are more likely to feel that you are speaking to them personally and politely and are thus more likely to do what you want.

Remember: Your reader should be able to *see* and *hear* you in your writing; just as you should be able to *imagine the reader* you are writing to.

GUIDELINE 17:

Put you and your reader into your writing.

Practice

Read each of the sentences below. Then rewrite the sentences in the spaces provided to make them sound more natural by including you, the writer, and your reader. You may make other changes to improve the readability of the sentences.

Example   The requirements for personal protective equipment are designed to guarantee the protection of workers from physical and chemical workplace hazards.

Rewrite   You are required to wear personal protective equipment to protect yourself from the physical and chemical hazards in our workplace.

The first three sentences in this exercise are from a company information sheet for new employees on required personal protective equipment.

1. Gloves are needed for protection from the weather.

_____

_____

2. The company requires footwear with shock-absorbing cushioned insoles for those of its employees who work on hard surfaces and stand for long periods of time.

_____

_____

3. Three observable effects of wearing respirators that employees need to be aware of are tiredness from the extra load, an inability to move as freely as they would without the respirators, and an inability to see as well or speak as clearly.

_____

_____

The next three sentences are from different health brochures written for the general public to tell them how to cope with various health problems, from cuts to measles to the common cold.

4. Healing is assisted when the wound and the affected skin are being kept dry.

_____

_____

5. The Rubella Elisa Test is recommended for a person who does not have a documented history of vaccination against rubella.

_____

_____

6. Cough medicine with codeine can be obtained from a pharmacy. A written prescription is not necessary.

_____

_____

UNNECESSARY WORDS

Why get rid of unnecessary words?

Unnecessary words spoil the readability of a document, and they can cloud the purpose. Be concise: say things once only, and say them in the fewest possible words. Here are some examples of wordy sentences and how to make them more concise.

Wordy	At this point in time, I am of the opinion that it is necessary that we install three new computer terminals.
Concise	We should install three computer terminals.
Wordy	There are several reasons for the decline in productivity.
Concise	Productivity has declined for several reasons.
Wordy	A decision was reached yesterday by the personnel department to review the hiring policy.
Concise	The personnel department decided yesterday to review the hiring policy.
Wordy	The reason I am writing this memo is to ask that you approve my request to take a management course.
Concise	I would like your approval to take a management course.
Wordy	The reaction will start when the solution is heated to a temperature of 77 degrees Celsius.
Concise	The reaction will start when the solution is heated to 77 degrees Celsius.

GUIDELINE 18:

Eliminate unnecessary words in your writing.

You can eliminate unnecessary words in your own writing by (1) eliminating wordy expressions; (2) eliminating repetition; (3) replacing verb-noun combinations with single verbs; and (4) beginning your sentences with the things or persons you're talking about.

Eliminating Wordy Expressions

Replace wordy expressions with concise ones whenever possible. Some examples are listed here:

TABLE 4.4
Readability blocks: wordy expressions

Change	To
a large number of	many
a long period of time	a long time
along the lines of	like
as a result of	because
at that particular time	then
at the present time	now
at this point in time	now
despite the fact that	although
due to the fact that	because
during the time that	while
for the purpose of	for
gain access to	get, obtain
in the amount of	for
in the event that	if
in the not too distant future	soon
is of the opinion	believes
it appears that	delete
it can be seen that	delete
it has been noted that	delete
it is necessary that we	we must
with reference to	about
with regard to	about

Eliminating Repetition

Avoid saying the same thing twice. The italicized parts of the following phrases and sentences are redundant and should be omitted:

My jacket is *of the colour* green.

The pool is rectangular *in shape*.

Our head office is in *the province of* Quebec.

I will return the report *back* to you after I've read it.

I know *for a fact* that the company plans to expand next year.

The building was *completely* destroyed by the fire.

The two offices were *exactly* identical.

The meeting starts at 9 a.m. *in the morning*.

This course covers the *basic* fundamentals of wordprocessing.

Could you please repeat that *again*?

final outcome

true facts

absolutely essential

in-depth study

completely eliminated

future plans

large *in size*

Replacing Verb-Noun Combinations with Single Verbs

Many wordy expressions are verb-noun combinations that could be replaced with single verbs. By using single verbs, you can eliminate some unnecessary words from your sentences.

TABLE 4.5
Readability blocks: verb-noun combinations

Change	To
advance an argument	argue
are in agreement with	agree
are of the opinion that	think
bring to completion	complete
came to the conclusion	concluded
come into conflict	conflict
come to a decision	decide
draw a conclusion	conclude
give assistance to	assist
give consideration to	consider
give instruction to	instruct
have a discussion	discuss
have a meeting	meet
make an adjustment in	adjust
make a concerted effort	try
make modifications to	modify
make a selection	select
take into consideration	consider

Beginning Your Sentence with the Things or Persons You're Talking About

You already learned in Chapter 2 that it's important to put the main idea at the beginning of each sentence. Putting the main idea at the start of a sentence produces a more direct and concise sentence. Avoid starting sentences with the phrases *There is…* and *It is….*

Put the subject of the sentence at the beginning; then find the real action of the sentence and express it as a verb:

Change	There are several problems with the new software.
To	The new software has several problems.
Change	It is necessary that we hire a new accounts manager.
To	We need to hire a new accounts manager.

 Practice

Read the following sentences carefully. Each sentence contains unnecessary words. Rewrite each sentence to improve its readability by taking out the unnecessary words. Be sure you keep the sense of the sentence.

Example	There are too many errors in this report.
Rewrite	This report has too many errors.

1. This report gives a comparison of the three candidates for the position of office manager.

   _____

   _____

2. A recommendation has been made as to who is best qualified for the position.

   _____

   _____

3. There were many factors that had to be taken into consideration before the personnel committee could reach a decision.

   _____

   _____

4. It is felt by the committee that Angela Liu is the most qualified candidate despite the fact that she doesn't have much experience in the building industry.

   _____

   _____

5. Fred Pirkey is not the best candidate for this position due to his lack of computer skills necessary to do the job.

    _____

    _____

6. At 10:30 a.m. this morning, a car that was green in colour was seen by me in collision with a van that was white in colour.

    _____

    _____

7. It is the opinion of this committee that we should give consideration to having a meeting in the not too distant future.

    _____

    _____

8. My reason for taking this course is to improve my computer programming skills.

    _____

    _____

9. I am writing this memo to let you know that I will be unable to attend next week's committee meeting due to the fact that I will have to give assistance to the new office manager in setting up for the Home and Gardens Show.

    _____

    _____

    _____

10. I have to give an oral talk in my Interior Design class.

    _____

    _____

11. Before I could complete the assignment, I had to re-read the chapter on operating systems again.

    _____

    _____

12. The reason why I want to attend the public meeting is to give my opinion on the proposal to add two lanes to Water Street.

    _____

    _____

13. I am of the opinion that we should hire a consultant to prepare the questions for the survey.

_____

_____

14. Please find enclosed a cheque in the amount of $50.

_____

_____

15. My office is in close proximity to the coffee shop.

_____

_____

MEASURABLE QUANTITIES

Information can be **measurable** or **non-measurable**. Non-measurable information is open to the reader's interpretation. Readers who need to know exactly what to do or exactly how a piece of information will affect them are often frustrated by non-measurable information. Imagine how frustrated you would be trying to follow instructions for a chemistry lab experiment that told you to "add some concentrated sulphuric acid." Imagine how much more likely your success if the instructions specified "5 mL of sulphuric acid."

The word *some* in "add some…acid" is imprecise because it can have many different meanings. One reader may interpret "some" to mean as few as 2 ml, while another reader may interpret "some" to mean as many as 200 ml. Here is a table of imprecise words that may frustrate readers:

TABLE 4.6
Readability blocks: imprecise words

Change	To
amount	lots, minimum of, maximum of
frequency	rarely, sometimes, often, frequently
probability	likely, unlikely, probable, certain
space	close, far
time	as soon as possible, soon, shortly, briefly

Practice

Here are some more examples of non-measurable and measurable information. Circle the imprecise words in the examples of non-measurable information.

Non-Measurable	The highway will be open shortly.
Measurable	The highway will be open in one to two hours depending on weather conditions.
Non-Measurable	Exercise regularly.
Measurable	Exercise three times a week for twenty to thirty minutes at a time.
Non-Measurable	Please contact me as soon as possible, so we can set a date for our next meeting.
Measurable	Please phone or e-mail me before 4:30 today, so we can set a date for our next meeting.

Measurable information is especially important when you're writing instructions:

Non-Measurable	Provide adequate space between the drier and the rear wall.
Measurable	Provide a minimum of 8 cm between the drier and the rear wall.
Non-Measurable	Monitor temperature and resistance.
Measurable	Record the temperature and resistance every 10 degrees Celsius, starting from 100 degrees Celsius.

GUIDELINE 19:

Replace imprecise words with specific and measurable information whenever possible.

REVIEW QUESTIONS

In your own words, answer the following questions.

1. Describe a simple test of readability.

   _____

   _____

2. Explain how using a plain and simple style will improve the readability of your writing.

   _____

   _____

3. Explain the advantages of putting you and your reader into your writing.

   _____

   _____

4. Explain how unnecessary words interfere with readability.

   _____

   _____

5. Describe measurable information.

   _____

   _____

PRACTICE WRITING ASSIGNMENT

Use the techniques you have learned so far in this textbook to improve the following letter. Use these effective writing techniques:

- Put the main idea first.
- Omit or replace readability blocks.
- Eliminate unnecessary words.
- Replace imprecise words with measurable information.
- Specify what action the reader should take.

MASON & DAUGHTER CONDOMINIUMS

15 Queen Street
Sault Ste. Marie, ON P6A 6K5

Mr. George Sneva
Tree Company
100 Industrial Park Crescent
Sault Ste. Marie, ON P6B 5P3

April 16, 199–

Dear Mr. Sneva

HORTICULTURAL SHIPMENT

An inspection of the horticultural shipment was carried out by our landscaping crew on April 15, 199—. With regard to the shipment, I have to inform you of the fact that there are some problems concerning the state of the aforementioned trees, since they all give the appearance of being totally dead. As well, it appears that although we received the correct number of silver maple, sugar maple, and red oak (although we were under the expectation they would be live trees), no yellow birch trees were in this shipment. Both of these problems should be taken care of in the near future.

These problems were reported by me via e-mail to Ms. Chu at your office on April 15. An agreement was reached that your company will arrange for the replacement of the dead trees with viable ones, and that the problem with the yews will also be appropriately resolved.

Please endeavour to carry out this work as soon as possible. It is necessary that we have the landscaping of these new condos completed by May 1, as we need to make preparations for our official opening in early May. Contact the under-signed regarding delivery of the replacements.

Sincerely

Catherine Mason

Catherine Mason

QUESTION SHEET

List any questions you have about this chapter.

Questions

_____

_____

_____

_____

_____

_____

_____

_____

_____

_____

_____

Answers

_____

_____

_____

_____

_____

_____

_____

_____

_____

_____

_____

_____

EXERCISES

Exercise 1: Using Measurable and Specific Information

NOTES FOR A PRESENTATION

Jean Gervais is a student enrolled in the International Trade program. She is compiling notes for a presentation on economic competition among nations. Here are Jean's notes:

> — *Canada is a very competitive nation.*
>
> — *Japan, the United States, Germany, and Switzerland are also among the most competitive nations in the industrialized world.*
>
> — *Among newly industrialized countries, the five most competitive are all located in Asia.*
>
> — *How well Canada is able to compete in the world markets of the 1990s and beyond will be affected by several factors.*

After reading her notes, Jean realizes that some of the information is vague; she'll need to re-read some of the journal articles she has consulted to add more specific information. Use the following information to help Jean add more measurable and specific information to her notes.

- Canada ranks as the industrialized world's fifth-most-competitive nation, according to the 1991 *World Competitiveness Report*. Japan is in first place. The United States is second, followed by Germany and Switzerland. Among the newly industrialized countries, Singapore is first. Hong Kong is second, followed by South Korea, Taiwan, and Malaysia.

- Factors that will determine how well Canada will be able to compete in world markets in the 21st century include the value of the dollar, interest rates, labour and manufacturing costs, research and development. A highly skilled workforce is probably the single most important factor.

Exercise 2: Using Measurable and Specific Information

THE WINTER SOLSTICE PARTY MEMO

Brian Pielak is office manager for a medium-sized engineering firm. Every year Brian sends out invitations to the annual staff Winter Solstice party. Every year the party is held at the Valley View Inn, where it has been held for the past five years. It's usually held on the third Friday in December. Anyone attending is asked to pay $15 to cover food costs. Brian decided that he would write only a short memo—just to remind people about the party. Here's the memo he wrote:

TO: All Staff

FROM: Brian Pielak, Office Manager

DATE: November 29, 199—

SUBJECT: An Invitation

You are invited to our annual staff Winter Solstice party. The party will be held in the usual place on Friday. It's sure to be as much fun as last year's party.

You can get a ride if you need one. Let me know soon if you're coming. I'll be collecting money soon. Hope to see you there.

The staff who joined the company this year have a few questions that the memo does not answer:

- When is the party?
- Where is the party?
- How much money?
- When will Brian collect the money?

Rewrite the memo for Brian by inventing and adding measurable and specific information, so new staff members can get all the necessary details. Be sure to also improve the subject line.

Exercise 3: Using Measurable and Specific Information

THE BIRTHDAY CAKE RECIPE

George and Lucia want to bake a birthday cake for a friend. George has an old family recipe, but he and Lucia are having trouble following it. The problem is not with George and Lucia's baking; the problem is with the recipe: the recipe has *no* measurable and specific information. Help Lucia and George by replacing the imprecise information in George's recipe with information that is measurable and specific.

Rewrite the recipe, so Lucia and George can follow it easily. Don't leave them with any questions. You may want to check your favourite cookbook or ask your friends for help.

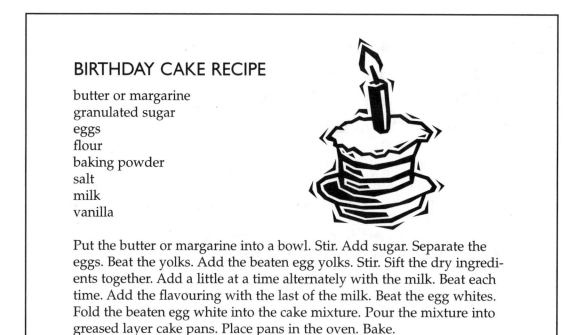

BIRTHDAY CAKE RECIPE

butter or margarine
granulated sugar
eggs
flour
baking powder
salt
milk
vanilla

Put the butter or margarine into a bowl. Stir. Add sugar. Separate the eggs. Beat the yolks. Add the beaten egg yolks. Stir. Sift the dry ingredients together. Add a little at a time alternately with the milk. Beat each time. Add the flavouring with the last of the milk. Beat the egg whites. Fold the beaten egg white into the cake mixture. Pour the mixture into greased layer cake pans. Place pans in the oven. Bake.

Exercise 4: Using Measurable and Specific Information

THE OFFICE BREAK-IN MEMO

Marieko Kaegi, assistant manager of ASAP Engineering, arrived at the office one morning to discover there had been a break-in. The office manager had a breakfast meeting and a series of appointments and wasn't expected in the office until noon. Marieko called the RCMP, and a Sergeant Pepper arrived to investigate. By 10 a.m. Marieko had everything under control. She left a report for the office manager and left for her 10:30 appointment out of town. Here's the memo she left:

TO: Richard Nelson, Manager

FROM: Marieko Kaegi, Assistant Manager

DATE: November 12, 199—

SUBJECT: A Problem at the Office

There was a break-in at the office. Some office equipment was stolen and some got damaged, but I took care of everything. I'll be in later to answer any questions.

M. K.

Marieko's report left Richard guessing: guessing what had been stolen and when, what had been damaged, and what Marieko had done about it. Rewrite the report for Marieko by adding measurable and specific information, so Richard doesn't have to guess. Don't forget to rewrite the subject line, which is also vague.

Exercise 5: Involving Your Reader

HANDOUT ON BICYCLE STORAGE AND MAINTENANCE

Helen Milajevic owns a small bicycle shop in Kingston. Her customers often ask her for tips on bicycle care and maintenance. During the five years she has been operating the store, Helen has written several short handouts for her customers on how to repair and maintain bicycles. She has just written part of a handout on "Storing Bicycles in the Winter." After reading it over, Helen notices that her writing sounds too impersonal; her sentences do not include people.

Help Helen put her readers into her writing. Rewrite the first part of her handout.

BICYCLE STORAGE AND MAINTENANCE

The storage place is usually determined by the housing situation. Depending on the amount of storage space in the home, it may be convenient to hang the bicycle by means of two hooks from the ceiling of the basement, garage, or storage closet. This writer finds winter a good time to disassemble the bike and clean all the parts. Some parts, like the chain, can be left in a container of oil for the winter. If the bicycle is totally disassembled, the re-assembly may provide a challenge in the spring. This shop can give bicyclists some tips on re-assembly should help be required.

Exercise 6: Involving Your Reader

INTRODUCTION TO "HOW TO USE A DISPOSABLE ESCAPE RESPIRATOR"

Canada is a major producer of pulp and paper. People from all over the world tour Canada's pulp and paper mills each year. When touring a pulp mill, each visitor must wear a hardhat and ear protection and carry a disposable escape respirator.

A disposable escape respirator, illustrated on the next page, is a mouth-bit respirator. The visitor carries the mask at all times. In case of a chemical leak in the mill buildings, the visitor puts on the mask (puts the "bit" or mouthpiece into her or his mouth) and thus can walk safely to the nearest exit. The respirator cannot be used more than once and therefore must be disposed of immediately after use.

Nikki is a process technician at a pulp mill. Her supervisor has asked her to prepare a handout on "How to Use a Disposable Escape Respirator" for all mill visitors. She is working on the introduction to her handout. In the introduction she wants to tell her readers when to use the escape respirator. She also wants to encourage them to read the instructions she has prepared. Nikki is happy with the content of her introduction, but she feels something is wrong. Her introduction sounds like she copied it from a book of government safety regulations. Nikki would like to involve her readers and use a more conversational tone.

Help Nikki put her readers into her writing. Rewrite Nikki's introduction, which follows.

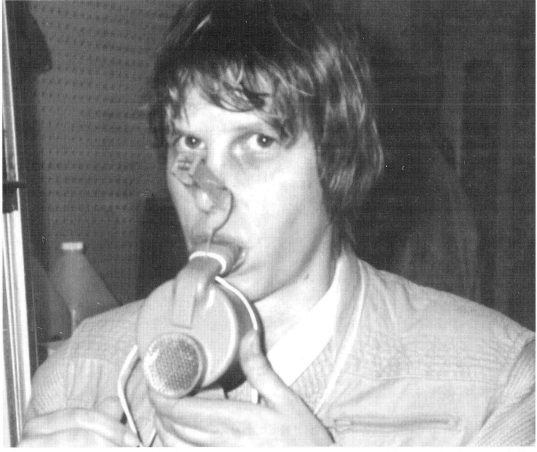

A disposable escape respirator

(photo by **David Kipling**)

HOW TO USE A DISPOSABLE ESCAPE RESPIRATOR: INTRODUCTION

Disposable escape respirators are to be carried by all visitors to the mill at all times. The escape respirators ensure the safety of all visitors in case of a gas leak. The respirators are to be worn as soon as the toxic gas alarm sounds or gas is suspected in the air. A burning or stinging sensation in the nose, mouth, or eyes is indicative of a situation that requires the use of escape respirators.

A disposable escape respirator is for evacuation purposes only. The respirator is to provide breathing protection while the wearer leaves by the nearest exit. The disposable escape respirator is disposable and should be used only once and should be discarded immediately after use. The cartridge, which filters contaminants from the air, is only effective for one use. Therefore, exhausted cartridges must be discarded.

A disposable escape respirator is designed for convenient carrying. The respirator can be clipped to a belt or hung from the neck.

A disposable escape respirator is designed for easy use. Reading the following instructions is all that is required to prepare the user should an emergency arise.

Exercise 7: Revising to Improve Readability

INSTRUCTIONS FOR "HOW TO USE A DISPOSABLE ESCAPE RESPIRATOR"

Now Nikki has written her instructions on "How to Use a Disposable Escape Respirator." Help her revise her instructions for readability. Eliminate any unnecessary words, replace imprecise words with measurable quantities, involve the reader, and replace words and expressions that are difficult to understand with plain, concise English.

HOW TO USE A DISPOSABLE ESCAPE RESPIRATOR

1. Remove the cover, which is made out of plastic, from the mouthpiece.
2. Hold the respirator in such a way that the mouthpiece is up and facing towards you.
3. Put the mouthpiece into the mouth, situating it so that it is located between the lips and the gums.
4. Bite down on the mouthpiece tabs, rubber extrusions, so as to effectively hold the mouthpiece in the mouth.
5. Put the nose clip on your nose.
6. Adjust the nose clip so that a nose seal is complete, with the nasal passages completely closed so it would be impossible for a person to breathe through the nose.
7. Breathe normally through the mouth.
8. Evacuate the contaminated area.

Exercise 8: Revising to Improve Readability

BICYCLE RACKS MEMO

Diane Michielli is vice-president of the student association at a college. The student association executive has asked her to write a memo to the college's head of security asking that additional bicycle racks be installed around campus.

Here is Diane's memo.

TO: Bob Makim, Security

FROM: Diane Michielli, Vice-President, Student Association

DATE: November 20, 199—

SUBJECT: Bicycle Racks on Campus

It is necessary that this college consider installing more bicycle racks for use by students and staff.

There are a large number of students who would appreciate having more bicycle racks. I happened to notice when I was taking a walk around campus just the other day that some students have to lock up bicycles inside buildings due to the fact that there are not enough bicycle racks. Some students just have to take a chance and leave their bicycles unlocked.

Subsequent to taking a walk around campus, I stopped by security to ascertain the number of racks situated on campus. I was informed that, at the present time, there are approximately thirty bicycle racks, with each rack's having a maximum capacity of six. It is felt by student council that a minimum of twenty racks need to be installed.

These racks could be situated in close proximity to the main buildings on campus. The racks could be fastened to walls or concrete by means of clamp devices, along the lines of the racks we are using at the current time.

More racks would provide adequate security for bicycles and ensure that none of the bicycles would be apprehended illegally. As I'm sure you know, there are already plenty of incidents of thievery around campus, and not just in our computer labs. As well, these racks would allow students and staff to utilize their bicycles for the purpose of going from one part of the campus to another.

Please give consideration to this request prior to the start of the fall session. Do not hesitate to contact me should you require further information or if you have any questions.

D. M.

Help Diane edit her memo for readability:

- Eliminate any unnecessary words.
- Replace imprecise words with measurable information.
- Eliminate any unnecessary details.
- Involve the reader.
- Replace words and expressions that are difficult to understand with plain, concise English.

You do not have to change the order of the sentences or the paragraphs.

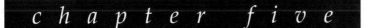

chapter five

ORGANIZING YOUR IDEAS
INTO PARAGRAPHS

As we wrote in the opening introduction, this book teaches you how to complete your school and workplace writing tasks correctly and efficiently. At school and work you can expect to be writing many reports, and at work you may write letters and memos as well. You already know that memos, letters, and reports are made of paragraphs. This chapter will teach you that paragraphs are not arbitrary blocks of print; they are groups of sentences that must be assembled with the same attention to your reader's needs that you used in choosing your words and composing your sentences. You will learn several practical ways to assemble your paragraphs.

Communication Outcomes

When you complete this chapter, you will be able to

- limit the length of each of your paragraphs to about seven typed lines
- use white space to help your readers see where one paragraph ends and the next begins
- begin each of your paragraphs with a main idea sentence that tells your reader what your paragraph is about
- explain the function of the main idea sentence in a paragraph
- develop your paragraph by adding any supporting details needed to answer your reader's questions about the main idea
- use supporting detail sentences in a paragraph to support the main idea of the paragraph in five ways:

  definition and clarification

  example

  comparison

  cause and effect (or effect and cause)

  classification and listing.

- lead your reader from your main idea sentence to your supporting sentences and from one supporting sentence to the next by using "signposts" and repeating key words
- plan your paragraphs
- evaluate your paragraphs, using given criteria.

Language Outcomes

When you complete this chapter, you will be able to

- write main idea sentences for your paragraphs
- write detail sentences that support your main idea sentences
- arrange detail sentences in a logical order that meets the reader's needs
- identify and use "signposts" for each of the five ways of explaining the main idea of a paragraph.

PARAGRAPH LENGTH

Paragraphs organize information. The more information you are giving your readers, the more important it is that you break down the information into manageable parts so your readers are not overwhelmed.

To make sure you write readable paragraphs, try and imagine your writing *visually* from the point of view of your readers. When your readers look at a page of writing, they see it helpfully organized into paragraphs. If the paragraphs are too long, however, they cease to be helpful and become obstacles to reading.

You can test this for yourself by looking at the information presented in the three paragraphs that follow.

A debit card is a bank or trust company card that allows you, while you're in a store, to immediately transfer the money for your purchase from your bank or trust account to that store's account. You will find paying with a debit card as easy as using a bank card. The store clerk will record the purchase on a point-of-sale terminal (what used to be called a cash register). The clerk will then sweep your debit card through the same device that is used to verify credit cards. Next, the clerk will hand you a keypad that works like a calculator. You will use the keypad the clerk gives you to key in your personal identification number or PIN. Your PIN will be the same as the one you key in when using your card at your bank machine. You will then, using the same keypad, verify the purchase amount and decide which of your bank accounts you want to debit for that amount.

The clerk will then hand you a transaction record along with your sales slip. Each transaction will cost you $1.25.

Confidentiality for all your transactions is ensured. Only you, not the store or the bank, know your PIN. While your bank statement will list all your debit card purchases, the store will not receive that list.

We bet you $1.25 we know which paragraphs you read first. We bet you read the second and third paragraphs first because those paragraphs were shorter and therefore the material *looked* easier. How many typed lines are in the second paragraph? How many typed lines are in the third paragraph? How many typed lines are in the first paragraph? Let's see what happens when we limit the length of each paragraph to seven typed lines or fewer. Read the five paragraphs below.

A debit card is a bank or trust company card that allows you, while you're in a store, to immediately transfer the money for your purchase from your bank or trust account to that store's account.

You will find paying with a debit card as easy as using a bank card. The store clerk will record the purchase on a point-of-sale terminal (what used to be called a cash register). The clerk will then sweep your debit card through the same device that is used to verify credit cards. Next, the clerk will hand you a keypad that works like a calculator.

You will use the keypad the clerk gives you to key in your personal identification number or PIN. Your PIN will be the same as the one you key in when using your card at your bank machine. You will then, using the same keypad, verify the purchase amount and decide which of your bank accounts you want to debit for that amount.

The clerk will then hand you a transaction record along with your sales slip. Each transaction will cost you $1.25.

Confidentiality for all your transactions is ensured. Only you, not the store or the bank, know your PIN. While your bank statement will list all your debit card purchases, the store will not receive that list.

This five-paragraph text gives *exactly* the same information as the preceding text. Notice how much easier it is to read several short paragraphs than one long one.

GUIDELINE 20:

Limit the length of your paragraphs to a maximum of about seven typed lines.

There is no minimum paragraph length—a one-sentence paragraph is perfectly acceptable. However, too many paragraphs of one or two sentences probably means you have not supported your ideas with enough detail. Do try to maintain a balance between long and short paragraphs. **Use short paragraphs of one or two sentences to catch your reader's eye and focus your reader's attention.**

You may wonder why we suggest seven lines as a maximum length for your paragraphs. In our experience seven typed lines is about the maximum-size block of typed words that the average person can read easily. If your paragraphs become much longer than seven typed lines, your readers will experience your writing as difficult to read.

GUIDELINE 21:

Use white space so your reader can see quickly and easily where each paragraph ends and the next paragraph begins.

Do not indent the first word of each paragraph. Instead begin the first word flush with your left-hand margin. **Leave one blank line between single-spaced paragraphs and four blank lines between double-spaced paragraphs.** We call this blank line "white space," since no print covers the white paper in that space.

Practice

Look back to the five paragraphs about debit cards. Quickly answer the following questions.

1. Which paragraph describes how easy it is to pay with a debit card? _____
2. Which paragraph is about confidentiality? _____
3. Which paragraph describes how the keypad is used?_____
4. Which paragraph defines debit card?_____

You probably took only about one minute to answer the four questions because *all* you had to read was the first sentence of each paragraph. In each instance the first sentence told you what the paragraph was about.

MAIN IDEA SENTENCE

GUIDELINE 22:

Begin each of your paragraphs with a main idea sentence that tells your reader what your paragraph is about. To complete your paragraph, add any supporting details needed to answer your reader's questions about the main idea.

Does this guideline sound familiar? It should. Your paragraphs should follow the same pattern you learned in Chapter 1: Identifying Your Reader and Purpose Before You Write, that is, put your main idea first and then add any supporting details needed to answer your reader's questions.

Likewise, each of your paragraphs, by beginning with the main idea, should follow the same pattern you also learned in Chapter 2: Putting Your Main Idea First in Every Sentence. In Chapter 2, you learned to tell your reader what your sentence was about right away, in the first few words.

The most important step you can take to become a successful writer is to put your main idea first—in your letters and memos (though you will learn a couple of exceptions), in your sentences, and in your paragraphs.

Let's look more closely at the function of the main idea sentence in a paragraph.

 ## Practice

Below is a main idea sentence for a paragraph. Read the main idea sentence and circle those words from the list below the sentence that you would expect to find in the rest of the paragraph.

Read the main idea sentence:

You can expect your hydroelectric bill to increase by at least $4.40 a month if you buy your own washer and dryer and do one load of laundry a day.

On the basis of the sentence above, which of the following words would you expect to see in the paragraph?

old frost-free refrigerator freezer

dollars ($)

microwave oven

clothes-washer

clothes-dryer

telephone bill

Here's the complete paragraph so you can check that you circled the right words.

You can expect your hydroelectric bill to increase by at least $4.40 a month if you buy your own washer and dryer and do one load of laundry a day. A clothes-dryer uses 960 kilowatt-hours of electricity a year, at a yearly cost of $48, based on one load a day. A clothes-washer uses 96 kilowatt-hours a year, at a yearly cost of $4.80, based on one load a day. You would have the additional cost of heating the water if you washed your clothes in hot or warm water. Thus, your yearly cost would be at least $52.80.

You probably found this exercise of circling the words very easy. That's because the function of a main idea sentence is to tell the reader what to expect. The main idea sentence is a contract or a promise you make to your reader to discuss that main idea, and only that main idea, in your paragraph. If you discuss any ideas in your paragraph that are not related to the main idea, your reader will be disappointed and confused, or annoyed with you for breaking your promise.

Notice the function of the remaining sentences in the paragraph: to support or explain the main idea. In the case of the paragraph on the increase due to running a washer and dryer, the remaining sentences explain the increase. As the writer explains in the supporting sentences, the causes for the $4.40 monthly increase are a $48 a year increase for running a dryer and a $4.80 a year increase for running a washer.

Practice

Here are three paragraphs missing their main idea sentences. For each paragraph, write a main idea sentence.

PARAGRAPH 1

Main Idea Sentence: _____

_____

_____

Supporting Details

- Hassiba Boulmerka needed to jump start her truck's engine, and she connected her battery to another truck's battery with booster cables.
- An electrical fault caused the booster cables to overheat and catch fire. The radiator grille and one headlight lens on Hassiba's truck were scorched.

PARAGRAPH 2

Main Idea Sentence: _____

_____

_____

Supporting Details

- The tires were made of rubber that deteriorated more quickly than usual in quarry use.
- The tire beads did fit the rims of our tractor wheels, as had been promised.
- The price, $15,000 per tire, was higher than that of any equivalent tractor tire for sale in Canada.

PARAGRAPH 3

Main Idea Sentence: _____

_____

_____

Supporting Details

- The first two calls listed were to Jamaica, with a total time of twenty minutes and a charge of $32.19. I have never telephoned Jamaica.
- The three calls to Thunder Bay of approximately five seconds each were wrong numbers.

WAYS OF DEVELOPING PARAGRAPHS

Now that you've learned how to write main idea sentences for your paragraphs, you'll need to learn how to support those main idea sentences with enough detail to meet your reader's needs. First, you'll learn five ways to support a main idea sentence in a paragraph. Then, you'll learn what order to use for your supporting detail sentences.

GUIDELINE 23:

Use supporting detail sentences in a paragraph to support the main idea of the paragraph in any one of five ways: definition and clarification; example; comparison; cause and effect (or effect and cause); and classification and listing.

Here is a a paragraph in which the main idea is supported through example.

> A kilowatt-hour (kW.h) is the amount of work done by one kilowatt of power operating for one hour; for example, a light-bulb rated at 100 watts, if left on for one hour, uses 100 watt hours of energy. In ten hours the light-bulb will use 1 000 watt hours or 1 kilowatt-hour.

Notice how the words "for example" in the paragraph above tell the reader that the writer is going to give an example to support the main idea. "For example" serves as a **signpost** leading the reader from the main idea to the supporting sentence. Signposts may also be used to lead the reader from one supporting sentence to the next.

Here is a table of the signposts for each of the five ways of explaining the main idea of a paragraph.

TABLE 5.1
Paragraph main idea

Way of Supporting the Main Idea	Signposts
Definition and clarification	to illustrate, in other words, that is, namely
Example	for example, for instance, specifically, in particular, such, such as
Comparison	like, unlike; in contrast; however; on the one hand, on the other hand; but; whereas; conversely; on the contrary; then, now; neither, nor; not, but; just as; similarly
Cause and effect (or effect and cause)	so, consequently, as a result, with the result that, therefore, thus, accordingly, thereby, for this reason, because, because of, owing to, due to, when, if
Classification and listing	as follows; furthermore; moreover; too; then; next; also; and; either, or; neither, nor; in addition; the other; various; one, two, three, etc.; first, second, third, etc.

Signposts are one way to lead your reader from one sentence of your paragraph to the next.

Another common way to connect sentences in a paragraph is the **repetition of key words**. Remember the exercise where you circled the words you expected to see in each paragraph after reading the main idea sentence? As you probably predicted, "clothes-washer," "clothes-dryer," and "dollars" were repeated in the paragraph. The repetition of those key words in the supporting detail sentences helps your reader to see the connection between the main idea sentence and the supporting details.

GUIDELINE 24:

Use signposts and repetition of key words in your paragraphs to lead your reader from your main idea sentence to your supporting sentences, and from one supporting sentence to the next.

Practice

You have learned that there are five ways of developing a paragraph: definition and clarification, example, comparison, cause and effect, and classification and listing. Look at the following five paragraphs and say which method each one uses.

You will find that most paragraphs you read are not developed purely in one way but often use one or more of the other ways as well. Write down the *major* method that the paragraph uses. To help you choose the major method, this exercise is designed so no two paragraphs use the same method.

PARAGRAPH 1

A screen saver is a piece of software that flashes changing images on your computer screen to prevent "burn-in." "Burn-in" is the damage that would happen to your screen if you left the same image on your monitor hour after hour, day after day.

Method: _____

PARAGRAPH 2

An example of a screen saver is the software called *Where have you gone?* This software contains ten animated messages for you to choose from. When you choose one of the ten messages, it will appear on your screen and then dissolve and refresh every few seconds. One such message, for example, is an "Out to Lunch" graphic, which has the words "Out to Lunch" on it and features a picture of a veggie burger and a cup of herbal tea. You can even add your own message to say, for instance, what time you will be returning from lunch.

Method: _____

PARAGRAPH 3

"Burn-in" occurs because your computer monitor is a cathode-ray tube (CRT), which uses an electron beam to draw a picture on the monitor screen. The electron beam draws the picture by striking a special phosphor coating on the inside of the screen. When the beam strikes the phosphor, it glows. This pattern of glowing phosphor forms the words or images you see. If you leave the electron beam aimed at just one part of the screen for a long time, the beam will eat away the phosphor coating at that location. As a result, the screen will cease to glow at that location.

Method: _____

PARAGRAPH 4
In contrast to a static image, such as a menu, the images provided by screen savers are constantly changing. Without a screen saver, most computers, whenever they are not in use, would show a menu listing the software available. This menu would cause "burn-in" since the image would be left on the screen at the same location for a long time. With screen savers, on the other hand, the electron beam is not constantly aimed at any one location. Thus, with screen savers, unlike with the menu, "burn-in" does not occur.

Method: _____

PARAGRAPH 5
Two solutions to the "burn-in" problem were considered. The first solution was to have the user turn off the monitor when the computer was not in use or, at least, to turn down the brightness. The brighter the image was on the monitor, the more apt the electron beam was to eat away the phosphor coating. The second solution was to encourage the user to install a screen saver.

Method: _____

Now go back to the five paragraphs in the preceding exercise. For each paragraph underline any signposts or repeated words that are used to lead the reader from the main idea sentence to the supporting detail sentence, and from one supporting sentence to the next.

Now it's your turn to write paragraphs using the five different methods.

PARAGRAPH PLANNING

GUIDELINE 25:

Plan each of your paragraphs by asking yourself the following:

- What is the main point of this paragraph? What do I want my reader to do or to know? Turn your answer into a main idea sentence.
- What must I next tell my reader to support my main point? Answer all your reader's questions. Turn your answers into supporting detail sentences.

Put your sentences in the logical order that most meets your reader's needs.
Always remember to arrange detail sentences in logical order.

The following two sample paragraphs announce their main ideas first, include the needed details, and arrange those details in a logical order that meets the reader's needs:

SAMPLE PARAGRAPH 1
Kyle Petty crashed his car on the one hundredth lap of the Daytona 500 race. Petty's car was following a group of three cars along the backstretch at 306 kilometres per hour. The first and second cars touched fenders and began to slide out of control. The third car braked to avoid the two sliding cars. Kyle Petty was so close to the third car that he hit it before he could brake. This collision caused Petty's car to swerve left off the track and on to the grass infield. Petty was unhurt, but his car could not be restarted to complete the race.

The details in the sample paragraph above describe the cause-and-effect sequence of the crash for a reader who, having read the main idea (a crash occurred), wants to know *how and why* it happened.

For a reader who wants instead to know the upshot or immediate results of the crash, the writer would write the paragraph differently:

SAMPLE PARAGRAPH 2

Kyle Petty crashed his car on the one hundredth lap of the Daytona 500 race. Petty, who was unhurt, was unable to complete the race because his car could not be restarted after the crash. Petty had hit a car that had braked suddenly to avoid two other cars spinning on the raceway.

Here the reader is less interested in the cause-and-effect sequence of events and more interested in the outcome.

 Practice

For the following five exercises, we will tell you enough about your reader so you can imagine what your reader will need to know. We will also tell you which method of paragraph development to use. Finally, we will give you all the information you will need.

Now, you write the paragraphs.

Topic: Campus Security

You are a member of the campus security committee, which is composed of students, non-teaching staff, teaching staff, and managers. At the next meeting of the committee, you want to propose that security install *indoor* emergency telephones. Currently the campus has only *outdoor* emergency telephones and indoor *service* telephones. Realizing that the other committee members may not be familiar with the existing emergency and service telephones, you decide to write a paragraph listing the types of telephones available now. You will then include this paragraph as background in your written proposal to be distributed before the meeting.

Here are your notes:

> — outdoor emergency telephones—will connect you immediately to security, without dialling, 24 hours a day, 7 days a week—cannot be used for any other local or outside calls
> — indoor service telephones installed in hallways-must dial the emergency telephone number 4357 (spells HELP) to contact security—can also be used for non-emergency calls to any local on campus and can also be used to dial 911
> — 16 outdoor emergency telephones on the campus walkways and in the parking lots-24 indoor service telephones in the hallways in all the campus buildings

Use the notes to write the paragraph listing the types of telephones currently available. Use the classification and listing method of paragraph development. Remember to write a main idea sentence at the beginning of your paragraph and use signposts.

Topic: Vancouver's Award-Winning Earthquake-Proof Building

You are a summer student working for the Architectural Institute of British Columbia, a non-profit association of architects that promotes the profession throughout the province. As part of its public education program, the institute is preparing a pamphlet on the ways in which structural engineers and architects have worked together to build amazing buildings.

Your supervisor has asked you to write a paragraph on the Westcoast Energy Building in downtown Vancouver. The Westcoast Energy Building was specially designed to withstand earthquakes. (The consulting engineer whose firm designed the building, Boguslaw Babicki, immigrated to Canada in 1958 from Poland. In 1971, his firm, Bogue Babicki and Associates, received both the American Iron and Steel Institute Design Award and the Canadian Consulting Engineer Award of Excellence for the Westcoast Energy Building.)

Your supervisor would like you to write one or two paragraphs comparing the Westcoast Energy Building with a conventional building.

Here is a picture of the Westcoast Energy Building, together with your rough notes:

Westcoast Energy Building

— concrete elevator core
— concrete elevator core supports the centre of the building
— cables embedded in the top of the concrete core reach out to the 4 corners of the top of the building
— cables thus support the perimeter of the building
— no columns
— central core is exposed at ground level—floors begin 3 storeys above ground level
— cost was 15 to 20 percent lower than conventional building
— like a tree

Conventional Building

— concrete elevator core
— concrete elevator core supports the centre of the building
— columns support the perimeter of the building
— floors usually begin at ground level, or if floors do not begin at ground level and the building is exposed underneath, columns would be visible outside the building
— cost is 15 to 20 percent higher than the Westcoast Energy Building
— like a box

Use the notes to write your paragraphs comparing the Westcoast Energy Building with a conventional building. Use the comparison method of paragraph development. Remember to write a main idea sentence at the beginning of each paragraph and use signposts.

Photograph courtesy of *Bogue Babicki and Associates*

Topic: Water Troubles in Gibsons

You work for the Town of Gibsons on the Sunshine Coast of British Columbia. You have tested the town water and found it slightly acidic, having a pH of 5.5 to 6.5. You need to write an official brochure for the residents of the town suggesting they run their taps for a short while each morning and take other measures to prevent harmful effects from the acidic water.

First, you must explain to the residents what you mean when you say the water is acidic.

After all, while some of the residents of Gibsons are graduates in Chemical Sciences and know all about pH, others have never heard of pH except what they know from TV commercials for shampoo to restore the hair's pH balance.

Here are some notes you jotted down:

> — Gibsons' water is soft and slightly acidic, pH 5.5 to 6.5
> — pH scale ranges from 0 to 14
> — the smaller the pH number, the more acidic the water
> — pure water is pH 7 or neutral pH
> — pH level is a measure of the level of acidity (how acidic something is)

Use the notes to write the paragraph explaining what you mean when you say Gibsons' water is acidic. Use the definition and clarification method of paragraph development. Remember to write a main idea sentence at the beginning of your paragraph and use the signposts.

Topic: Water Troubles in Gibsons (Continued)

You decide the residents could use some examples to help them understand pH and acidity. Here are your notes:

> — ammonia—pH 12
> — lemon juice—pH slightly less than for vinegar
> — baking soda—pH 8
> — average pH of rainfall in Toronto (in 1979)—pH 3.5
> — "clean rain"—pH 5.5
> — vinegar—slightly less than pH 3
> — apple juice—pH 3
>> pH 7 — neutral
>> pH higher than 7 to 14 — increasingly alkaline
>> pH lower than 7 to 0—increasingly acidic

Use the notes to write the paragraph giving examples of pH and acidity. Use the example method of paragraph development. Remember to write a main idea sentence at the beginning of your paragraph and use signposts.

Topic: Water Troubles in Gibsons (Conclusion)

You are ready to tell the residents what to do about the acidic water. You know the residents are more apt to do as you ask if you explain why. For each action you want the residents to take, you've jotted down some reasons. You realize you may have to write *two or three paragraphs* instead of just one.

Here are your notes:

Run taps for two minutes in the morning until the water turns cold.

— older copper pipes often are joined using lead solder

— in the morning the water will be stagnant in the pipes

— heavy metals dissolve more easily in acidic water

— taps are usually not used all night

— if water remains stagnant in the pipes, it will dissolve the lead

— lead is a heavy metal

Do not use water from the hot water tap for cooking or for making tea.

— use water from the cold tap

— metals dissolve more easily in hot water than in cold water

Do not use aluminum cookware, lead crystal cups, or ceramic mugs with lead glaze.

— aluminum dissolves more easily in acidic water

— lead dissolves more easily in acidic water

— ceramic mugs may have lead in their glazing

Use the notes to write your paragraphs. Use the cause-and-effect method of paragraph development. Begin each of your paragraphs with a main idea sentence and use cause and effect statements to tell your readers why you want them to do something.

PARAGRAPH EVALUATION

Now, evaluate the paragraphs you have written.

Evaluate your paragraphs by asking these questions:

1. Is your main idea in the first sentence of each paragraph? Does the first sentence state what you want your reader to do or to know?

2. Have you included enough supporting details to explain the main idea to your reader? Do you leave your reader with unanswered questions? If you do, answer them. Are the supporting details arranged in a logical order that meets your reader's needs?

3. Is there anything in your paragraph that is *not* related to the main idea? If there is, take it out.

4. Does your paragraph have a maximum of about seven typewritten lines? If your paragraph has more than about seven lines, divide your paragraph into two or more paragraphs with their own main idea sentences.

5. Have you used signposts or repeated key words to lead your reader from one sentence to the next?

6. Have you followed the rules you learned in chapters 2 through 4 of this book for choosing your words carefully and writing effective sentences?

REVIEW QUESTIONS

In your own words, answer the following questions.

1. Why is it important to limit the length of a paragraph?

2. What is white space, and why do you use it around your paragraphs?

3. What are signposts, and what do they do for your reader?

4. How do you decide what order to use for your supporting details?

5. List five ways to develop the main idea in a paragraph. List two signposts you could use for the supporting details for each of the five ways.

6. In this book you've learned to plan before you write. Explain how to plan your paragraphs.

PRACTICE WRITING ASSIGNMENT: ORGANIZING DETAILS INTO EFFECTIVE PARAGRAPHS

REPORT ON AN ACCIDENT

Organize the details listed below into effective paragraphs. Begin each paragraph with a main idea sentence, and arrange the supporting details in a logical order that meets your reader's needs. Use signposts and the repetition of key words to connect the sentences within your paragraphs.

Use the plan sheet to help you organize your paragraphs. Then, write the information up as a memo report. After you've checked your own paragraphs according to the evaluation sheet in the section Evaluating Your Paragraphs, revise your report as necessary. Then, give the memo report and the plan sheet to your teacher for evaluation.

The details listed below are notes hastily scribbled by a technician for an Agriculture Canada lab, whose day turned sour when he crashed the lab car in the vineyards. After going to the doctor and having the car towed, he went back to the lab to speak to his section head. She told him to fill out a report on the accident.

Pretend you're the technician, and based on the notes, write a brief report of the accident.

Your purpose in writing is to report the details of the accident. Your reader is the section head of the Agriculture Canada lab where you work.

1. accident date—July 15th

2. company car #19—1997 Dodge Chrysler Neon, Licence No. MT 2241

3. on way to the experimental plot in Martha's Vineyard

4. was driving through Martha's Vineyard in the field southwest of the cemetery

5. to check experiment on the effect on growth of the mechanical tying of vines

6. slid off the dirt road and into the end support-post for the wires the grapes grow on

7. time: 2 p.m. (approximately)

8. irrigation system had been running on the previous night, so road had been soaked

9. soil was silty—it's clay loam—slippery and greasy

10. vehicle damage: rear quarter panel on the passenger side is totalled

11. end support-post in vineyard: also totalled

12. I received bruises, cut on forehead

13. called tow truck from cemetery office

14. phoned in accident details to section head—3 p.m.

15. got ride with tow truck to my doctor

16. car towed to the service station, corner of Holly Wood and Vine

17. called the service station: panel replacement estimated at $800

18. the researcher I was working for on this experiment had an accident last summer at the exact same spot

19. I was driving in second gear at 20-25 km per hour when the accident occurred

20. doctor says no potential problems with bruises or cut

Plan Sheet for the Practice Paragraph Assignment

Follow these six steps to fill out the plan sheet:

1. Group your details (the twenty notes). One way to do this is to go down the list of twenty items in order. Put a star next to the first item. Then, go down the list, and whenever you see an item that belongs with the first item, mark it too with a star until you come to the end of the list.

   Then, go back to the first item on the list that you *haven't* marked with a star. Mark that item with a triangle. Go down the list, marking with a triangle each item that belongs. Continue this process, using a different symbol each time (circles, diamonds, etc.), until you've grouped all the items on the list.

2. Recopy each group of details on to the plan sheet below. You could, for example, recopy the details you marked with triangles in the first details section of the plan sheet.

3. Name each group of details. Ask yourself, for example, "What are all the triangle items about?" and "What are all the circle items about?" Write the names in the spaces provided on the plan sheet. If you can't name a group, see if the details should be re-allocated to other groups.

4. For each group of details, ask yourself, "What is the main idea I want my reader to know about this group of details?" The name you've given your group will help you answer this question. Turn the answer to this question into a main idea sentence. Write the sentence in the space provided on the plan sheet.

5. For each group, cross out any notes that are now also in your main idea sentence. Number the remaining details to answer your reader's questions in the order in which those questions will occur to your reader.

6. Number the groups of details according to the order in which your reader will need to hear them.

Details: _____

_____

_____

_____

_____

_____

_____

Name of Group: _____

_____

Main Idea Sentence: _____

_____

Details: _____

_____

_____

_____

_____

_____

_____

Name of Group: _____

_____

Main Idea Sentence: _____

_____

Details: _____

_____

_____

_____

_____

_____

Name of Group: _____

_____

Main Idea Sentence: _____

_____

Details: _____

_____

_____

_____

_____

_____

Name of Group: _____

_____

Main Idea Sentence: _____

_____

QUESTION SHEET

List any questions you have about this chapter.

Questions

_____

_____

_____

_____

_____

_____

_____

_____

_____

_____

_____

Answers

_____

_____

_____

_____

_____

_____

_____

_____

_____

_____

_____

EXERCISES

Exercise 1: Ordering Sentences in Paragraphs

LETTER TO ACCOMPANY A COMPANY CATALOGUE

Lee Teng-hui's company in Taipei exports hardware around the world. Lee Teng-hui has written a letter to accompany a copy of the company catalogue he is sending to potential customers around the world. Below are the ten sentences that constitute Teng-hui's letter. The sentences are out of order. Rewrite the sentences so they are in correct order and form four separate paragraphs. You do not have to change the sentences or add any words. You need only change the order of the sentences and divide them into paragraphs.

1. Enclosed are our catalogue and quotations of prices.
2. If you have any questions or need any further information, please write me or call me at (02) 715-1575.
3. We have exported hardware to the United States for twenty years.
4. Our ordering service, which includes telephone, telex, fax and e-mail, allows you to place your order quickly and efficiently.
5. Since my company is the leading exporter in Taiwan, we should consider doing business with one another.
6. We look forward to doing business with you.
7. Mr. Peter Tom, vice-president of the Bank of America in Taipei, can testify as to our credit and stable position in the world business community.
8. I read your advertisement in the *Wall Street Journal* in which you introduced yourself as the "leading importer in the U.S." and mentioned your plans to buy hardware in Asia.
9. Our reputation for good price and high quality is well established; our exports to America total more than U.S. $1,000,000 a month.
10. My company can offer you hardware of outstanding quality at a reasonable price.

Insert the following at the beginning of your letter:

Lung Meng Exporting Co., Ltd.

2F, No. 41, Alley 28, Lane 688,
Min Sheng East Road
Taipei, Taiwan

July 1, 199—

E. Z. Bolt Imports, Inc.
250 West 57th Street, Room 1321
New York, NY 10107
U.S.A.

Close your letter as follows:

LEE TENG-HUI, DIRECTOR OF MARKETING

Enclosures: 2

Exercise 2: Identifying Signpost Words and Phrases

AC AND DC CURRENT

As you learned earlier in this chapter, you can use signposts (for example, because, but, next, etc.) to lead your reader from one sentence of your paragraph to the next. This chapter also contains a table of signpost words and phrases.

Don't force the use of these words, but use them when they will strengthen the paragraph; used correctly, signposts should link your sentences and help your reader move quickly through the material.

Below are some paragraphs on AC and DC electric current. Working with a partner, you should underline the words or phrases that serve as signposts. Then discuss the meaning of the underlined words, how they link ideas, and how the sentences are punctuated.

WHAT ARE AC AND DC?

AC is alternating electric current and DC is direct electric current.

Although AC has more applications in modern life, electricity was first used in DC form. In 1886, George Westinghouse experimented with alternating current because it could be sent over longer distances. As a result, it was more practical than direct current.

To produce alternating current, you need a wire and a magnet. One of these must move past or spin around the other. As it does, the poles of the magnet force electrons through the wire, causing an electric current to flow. Because the north and south poles of the magnet keep changing as they spin past the wire, the current reverses direction, or alternates, periodically.

If your eyes were fast enough, you could see your lights dim and brighten as the magnetic poles alternate. But the poles alternate sixty times each second, and the human eye is capable of seeing only about sixteen cycles per second.

AC is more commonly used today; however, DC still has many applications. For example, batteries for flashlights, transistor radios, cameras, and automobiles use DC. As well, new technologies permit DC voltage as high as 500,000 volts for long-distance transmission.

Exercise 3: Adding Signpost Words and Phrases

THE EXHIBITION AREA MEMO

You are assistant to Alain Charlebois, general manager for Coconut Grove, Inc., a medium-sized company that specializes in manufacturing and distributing hot tubs. The company is based in Calgary, Alberta. Currently, the company distributes its products mainly in Alberta, Saskatchewan, and Manitoba, but recently it decided to set up a retail and distribution outlet in Peterborough, Ontario.

Both you and Alain recently attended the annual Spring Home and Garden Show at Exhibition Centre, located in downtown Toronto. While at the exhibition, you and Alain checked out the displays of competing companies and also spent some time at Coconut Grove's exhibit area.

Both of you noticed a couple of problems that could affect your sales at future exhibitions. Back at the office in Calgary on Monday morning, Alain asked you to write a memo to all staff about the problems you saw at the exhibition.

Here is the memo:

TO: All Sales, Finance, and Distribution Staff
FROM: Alain Charlebois, General Manager
DATE: March 3, 199—

Coconut Grove's Exhibition Area at the Spring Home and Garden Show: Toronto, ON, February 25-28

Coconut Grove's first-ever exhibition at the Spring Home and Garden Show was very successful. We received more than one hundred orders for our newest models. We should consider ways to solve two problems before next year's Home and Garden Show.

The size of our area at the spring show was about 275 square metres, the same size as our exhibition area at the Calgary Home Show. We added two new models to our line this year. This made our exhibition area seem very crowded.

Several of our West Coast competitors had exhibit areas of 365 to 457 square metres. We were all in the same section of Exhibition Centre. It was easy to see we were making a poor impression on our potential customers.

Our exhibit area was staffed by only one sales representative. Some potential customers left the exhibit because they had to wait too long to talk with the rep.

I suggest the following. Next year we should increase the size of our exhibit area to 365 square metres to ensure there is enough room for the new models and to give customers enough room to view the hot tubs. We should make sure there are at least two sales representatives available at all times to handle questions from customers.

Please consider these suggestions before our next weekly meeting.

A. C.

After reading the draft of your memo, you realize that you need to add some words and phrases to link the sentences together.

Help your readers move quickly through the ideas in the memo by adding signpost words and phrases between and within sentences.

You do not have to change the order of the sentences or the paragraphs. You have only to add words or phrases.

Exercise 4: Organizing Paragraphs

This exercise has two parts. In Part 1, you will revise a memo written to request representatives for a health and safety committee. In Part 2, you will revise a memo announcing a schedule for resurfacing driveways.

MEMO REQUESTING REPRESENTATIVES FOR A HELATH AND SAFETY COMITTEE

Here is a draft of a memo written to employees at A. H. Samanez, a large engineering consulting firm with offices in Toronto, Montreal, and Vancouver.

The sentences in the memo are in the correct order, but they need to be divided into paragraphs. Some of the sentences need to be rewritten. Revise the memo, so that there are at least four paragraphs. Each paragraph should be about one main idea.

TO: Managers, All Departments

FROM: Leslie Macleod, Manager, Occupational Health and Safety

DATE: August 3, 199—

REPRESENTATIVES NEEDED FOR OCCUPATIONAL HEALTH AND SAFETY COMMITTEE

Could you please send me a list of the names of the people in your department who would be willing to serve on the company's occupational health and safety committee. We will need a total of eight committee members, one member from each department. Committee members meet once a month and also take part in safety inspections and accident investigations. Each committee member will also be asked to visit a particular area of one of our three main locations once a month to investigate workplaces and determine if any hazardous conditions exist. Members can also act as liaisons between their co-workers and the safety and security department. The function of the committee is to promote health and safety throughout the company and to encourage employee participation in making this company a safe place to work. Call me if you have any questions about this request or if you would like me to meet with your department to talk more about the role of committee members. Please e-mail your list of names to me by the end of September, so I can contact new members before October 7, the next scheduled meeting of the occupational health and safety committee.

L. M.

Some Additional Information on Health and Safety Committees

An occupational health and safety committee is a joint committee of worker and employer representatives working together to identify and resolve safety and health problems in the workplace.

The committee may be a requirement of the industrial health and safety regulations of your provincial Workers' Compensation Board, depending on the number of employees and the type of industry.

Use the following format for your memo:

TO: Managers, All Departments

FROM: Leslie Macleod, Manager, Occupational Health and Safety

DATE: August 3, 199—

REPRESENTATIVES NEEDED FOR
OCCUPATIONAL HEALTH AND SAFETY COMMITTEE

MEMO ANNOUNCING THE SCHEDULE FOR RESURFACING DRIVEWAYS

Here is a draft of a memo from a property management company to residents at a townhouse complex. The sentences are in the correct order, but they need to be divided into paragraphs. Some of the sentences need to be rewritten. Revise the memo, so that there are at least four paragraphs. Each paragraph should be about one main idea.

DRAFT MEMO

The driveways in your complex are scheduled to be resurfaced starting on Monday, August 10, and finishing Saturday morning, August 22. The resurfacing is scheduled as follows: Monday, August 10, house numbers 3872 to 4270 beginning at 9 a.m. and ending at 6 p.m. Wednesday, August 12, house numbers 4271 to 4320 beginning at 9 a.m. and ending at 3 p.m. Friday, August 14, house numbers 4321 to 4530 from 9 a.m. to 4 p.m. Saturday, August 22, house numbers 4530 to 4537 from 7 a.m. to 1 p.m. or until the work is completed. You will have to park on the street while your driveway is being resurfaced. As well, please remove all items from your driveway, including bicycles and planters. If you will be out of town while the driveways are being resurfaced and plan to leave your vehicle in the driveway, please leave your car keys with a neighbour, so that your car can be moved. Please call Joanna Krzesinski at Stratagrow at 763-3302 if you have any questions.

Use the following format for your memo:

TO:	All Residents, Fairway Estates
FROM:	Joanna Krzesinski, Stratagrow Management
DATE:	August 3, 199—
SUBJECT:	Schedule for Driveway Resurfacing

Exercise 5: Using Comparison Structures

This exercise will give you practice in using **comparison** to support the main idea of a paragraph. When you compare, you examine two or more items to discover their similarities and differences.

In the business world, companies often use comparisons when they are looking for solutions to problems. If, for example, a small accounting firm wants to buy some accounting software but can't decide which software package will best meet its needs and budget, the manager of the firm may be asked to write a report comparing several software packages for cost, ease of use, and functions.

Technologists compare unfamiliar objects with familiar ones to help define size, shape, and location; for example, saws have teeth, screws have heads, and roads have shoulders.

Business and technical magazines sometimes compare and contrast new components and devices for readers interested in comparing several models of a product.

Speaking

Working with a partner, compare *orally* the items in each of the following pairs. You should use one or two sentences for each comparison. A good way to make a comparison is to begin with those factors the two items have in common. Include at least one way the two items are similar and one way they are different. Use the signpost words and phrases you learned about in this chapter.

- a portable computerized spell-checker and a dictionary
- a video camera and a 35-mm camera
- an electronic burglar alarm system and a guard dog

Writing

By yourself, write one or two sentences comparing the items in each of the above pairs. Use signposts to connect your sentences.

a portable computerized spell-checker and a dictionary

_____

_____

_____

a video camera and a 35-mm camera

_____

_____

_____

an electronic burglar alarm system and a guard dog

_____

_____

_____

Exercise 6: Writing Comparison Paragraphs Using Information in a Table

Why Writers Use Tables for Business and Technical Writing

Comparisons can be made in several ways. In the previous exercise, you wrote sentences to compare the items. Sometimes you can use a table to help your readers see comparisons quickly; a table can show certain kinds of information and relationships, although not all, more clearly and concisely than words alone.

Many of the textbooks you will read, and some of your reports and presentations, will contain tables. We have used tables throughout this book, as you can see.

Here is an excerpt from a report comparing three models of notebook computers. In this section of the report, the writer uses a table to show the similarities and differences among the three models.

COMPARISON OF THREE NOTEBOOK COMPUTERS

Table 3.1 compares three models of notebook computers:

1. Superdata 7000
2. Takedo BF-65
3. Millen 2001

All three models use a Windows 95 operating system, which is compatible with our desktops. As well, all weigh between 3 and 3.5 kilograms, so they'll be easy to carry.

As we agreed when we met in November, the most important criteria for us in selecting a notebook computer are

- CPU: Pentium 200 processor
- Memory: minimum 32 MB RAM
- Storage Capacity: minimum 2.1 GB hard drive, CD-ROM drive, floppy drive
- Screen Size: minimum 30-centimetre screen
- Warranty: minimum two years
- Price: maximum $6,000.

Here is some background information on the terms used in this exercise:

Central Processing Unit (CPU): The CPU is like the computer's engine. It carries out the instructions of a computer program. Some examples of computer programs are Microsoft Word and Windows 95.

Memory (also referred to as RAM, which stands for random access memory): Memory stores a temporary copy of your computer programs and data, so they can be quickly retrieved by the CPU. In contrast to memory, the hard drive stores your computer programs and data permanently.

The higher the RAM number, the more information that can be held; for example, 64 MB (megabytes of) RAM holds twice as much information as 32 MB RAM. Most offices would need to have computers with at least 32 MB RAM.

Storage Capacity: Storage capacity refers to the amount of information you can save on a hard drive, a CD-ROM, or a floppy drive. Most offices would need to buy computers with at least 2 GB (gigabytes).

Gigabyte (GB): One GB is equal to 1 billion bytes. A 2.1 GB hard drive can store 2.1 billion bytes. One byte is equal to 8 bits. A bit is equivalent to the amount of energy it takes to turn a light-bulb on or off.

Following is the table that the writer included in the report:

Table 3.1
Comparison of notebook computers

Specifications	Superdata 7000	Takedo BF-65	Millen 2001
CPU	Pentium 200	Pentium 200	Pentium 200
Memory	64 MB RAM	32 MB RAM	64 MB RAM
Storage capacity	hard drive: 3.1 GB CD-ROM drive floppy drive	hard drive: 2.1 MB CD-ROM drive floppy drive	hard drive: 2.1 MB CD-ROM drive floppy drive
Screen size	31 cm	31 cm	31 cm
Warranty	3 years	3 years	1 year
Price	$5,074	$5,999	$6,100

Discuss the following questions with a partner or the other members of your group:

Similarities

1. How are all three models alike?
2. How is the Superdata 7000 like the Millen 2001?
3. How is the Superdata 7000 like the Takedo BF-65?

Differences

1. How is the Superdata 7000 different from the Takedo BF-65?
2. How is the Takedo BF-65 different from the Millen 2001?
3. How are all three models different from one another?

Writing from a Table

Using the information from the table comparing the three notebook computers, write one or two paragraphs in which you compare the three models according to the specifications listed in the table.

Exercise 7: Putting Information into a Table

Tables are also used in science and business as a way of organizing information. Look through one of your science textbooks for examples of tables. You can also look at the tables we have used throughout this textbook for examples of how to set up tables.

Imagine you're reviewing some notes you made while you were listening to a lecture on the physical properties of common metals. You realize your notes are jumbled and hard to study from. You decide to put the information into a table so you can see comparisons quickly. Here are your notes:

— Iron has a high boiling point, 2 730 degrees Celsius and a melting point of 1 528 degrees Celsius.

— Iron has a specific gravity (weight) of 7.85-7.88. Cobalt has a specific gravity of 8.9, nickel has 8.90, and copper is 8.93-8.95.

— Cobalt and nickel have the same boiling point—2 900 degrees Celsius.

— Cobalt has a melting point of 1 495 degrees Celsius.

— Nickel doesn't have the same melting point as cobalt. Nickel has a melting point of 1 455 degrees Celsius.

— Iron has a melting point of 1 528 degrees Celsius. Copper has the lowest melting point of these four metals—1 083 degrees Celsius.

— Copper also has the lowest boiling point—2 336 degrees Celsius.

Working with a partner, put the information from your notes into a table. Give your table a title. After you've completed the table, make comparisons (orally) that express the similarities and differences among the metals. Use some of these words and phrases in your comparisons:

— heavier than

— lighter than

— as high as

— not as high as

— the highest

— the lowest

— lower than

— as low as

— like

— compared with

— equal

— similar

— identical.

Exercise 8: Writing Paragraphs for Which You Are Given Information

For this exercise, you will be given all the information you need to write paragraphs on saving energy in your garage.

SAVING ENERGY IN YOUR GARAGE

You work in the technical department at Northwood Pulp Mill in Prince George. As part of its growing interest in the environment, your company encourages employees to submit short articles for the company newsletter on how to save energy both at home and at work. You decide to write a paragraph or two on how people can save energy in their garages by using timers on the block heaters to warm up their car engines.

While you're making notes for your paragraph, a colleague, who's looking over your shoulder, suggests you also add a paragraph about power-saver cords. You agree to write one more paragraph.

Because of the cold climate, many people in Prince George leave block heaters plugged into the engine blocks of their cars all night. A block heater keeps the engine warm, so that it will start easily. A block heater also saves on gas, since less fuel is required to start a warm engine than a cold engine. Although block heaters do not need to be on all night for the engines to be warm in the morning, people turn the block heaters on before they go to bed at night because they certainly aren't going to get up in the middle of the night just to turn on the block heaters.

In your short article, you want to suggest that people use timers on their block heaters. In addition, you'd like to suggest that they consider using power-saver cords instead of timers. For those of you who have never lived in cold climates, we've included illustrations of a block heater, timer, and power-saver cord. You will not need to put this information in your paragraph since people in Prince George are already familiar with these devices; we have only included them as background for you.

We have also included notes that will give you the information on timers and power-saver cords that you need to write your paragraphs.

Figure 5–1

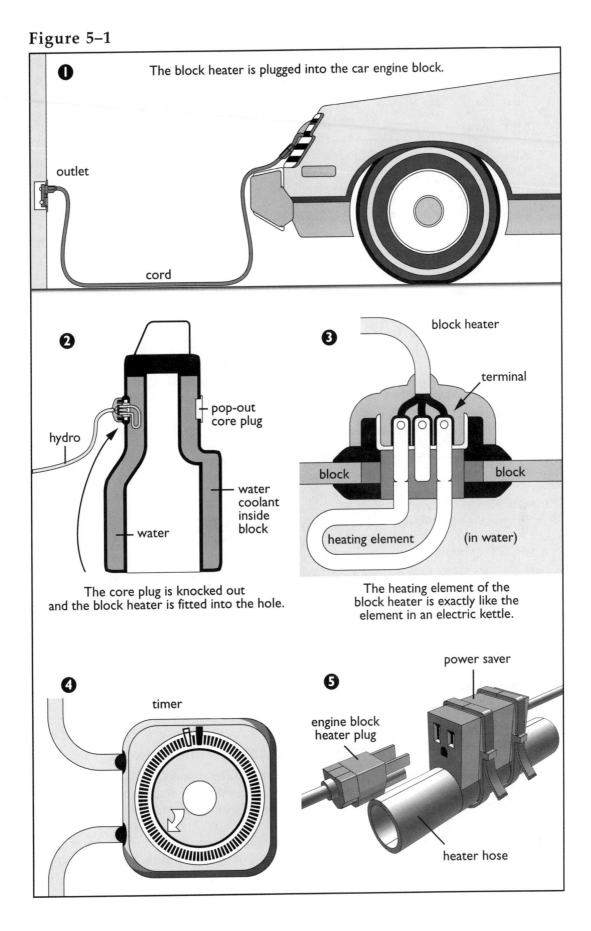

❶ The block heater is plugged into the car engine block.

outlet

cord

❷

hydro

pop-out
core plug

water
coolant
inside
block

water

The core plug is knocked out
and the block heater is fitted into the hole.

❸ block heater

terminal

block

block

heating element

(in water)

The heating element of the
block heater is exactly like the
element in an electric kettle.

❹ timer

❺ power saver

engine block
heater plug

heater hose

Notes on Timers and Block Heaters

— Timer—set to turn on the block heater about three hours before you need to leave for work. That's all the time needed to warm engine.

Appliance	Nightly kW.h Used	Nightly cost $
500-watt block heater without timer (left on for 12 hours)	6	.36
500-watt block heater with timer (left on for 3 hours)	1.5	.09

NOTES ON POWER-SAVER CORD

— Another way to control the costs of running your block heater.

— Extension cord with a thermostat built into it.

— Is mounted on the top radiator hose, as close as possible to the engine block.

— Block heater is plugged into the mounted end of the power-saver cord.

— The thermostat is inside the mounted end of the power-saver cord.

— Can't give specific numbers (e.g., of kW.h used and nightly cost) because the energy used depends on the outside temperature and wind conditions. The power-saver cord turns off the power whenever the temperature exceeds -7 degrees Celsius, so how long the block heater is on depends upon the surface temperature of the radiator hose, which is affected by the weather.

— Minus 7 degrees Celsius is the recommended minimum temperature for starting an engine.

— With the power-saver cord, the block heater is only switched on when the engine temperature drops below minus 7 degrees Celsius.

Exercise 9: Writing Paragraphs for Which You Are Given the Information

For this exercise, you will be given all the information you need to write paragraphs on saving energy in an apartment building.

SAVING ENERGY IN A SEVENTEEN UNIT APARTMENT BUILDING

Kathy Center runs an apartment maintenance service. The owners of Pleasant Gardens Apartments have asked her to calculate the savings they could realize by switching to energy-saving fluorescent lighting for their hallway, exit, and external lighting in the seventeen-unit apartment building.

Kathy inspected the building's present lighting system, which uses incandescent light-bulbs, and calculated the costs of operating the present system and those of operating a fluorescent lighting system. Here are her figures:

PRESENT SYSTEM: QUANTITY AND WATTAGE OF LIGHTING ANNUAL OPERATING COST

40 x 60 watt hallway fixtures—on 24 hrs. a day	$1,051.20
21 x 60 watt external fixtures—on 12 hrs. a day	275.94
36 x 25 watt emergency exit bulbs—on 24 hrs. a day	394.20

Total Annual Cost $1,721.34

PROPOSED NEW SYSTEM: QUANTITY AND WATTAGE OF LIGHTING ANNUAL OPERATING COST

40 x 13 watt fluorescent tubes—on 24 hrs. a day	$222.76
21 x 13 watt fluorescent tubes—on 12 hrs. a day	59.51
36 x 7.5 watt emergency exit bulbs—on 24 hrs. a day	118.26

Total Annual Cost $405.53

Kathy plans to send Pleasant Gardens her figures, but she would also like to include an explanation in one or two paragraphs. She realizes that not everyone knows that an incandescent light-bulb is a "normal" light-bulb, so she will need to include that information. She has jotted down the following notes on incandescent bulbs and fluorescent tubes:

— *Fluorescent lighting uses less than one-quarter the electricity to produce the same amount of light as incandescent lighting.*

— *Fluorescent lighting does not waste as much energy on heat.*

— *An incandescent 60-watt bulb produces 860 lumens; a 13-watt fluorescent tube produces 900 lumens.*

(Lumen: a unit of light intensity)

Write one or more paragraphs for Kathy to put in her letter, along with her figures on the present and proposed new system, to the owners of the apartment building. Your paragraphs should summarize and explain the results of Kathy's study of the present and proposed lighting systems at Pleasant Gardens.

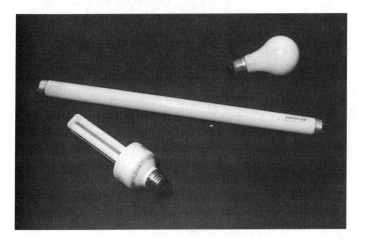

Exercise 10: Writing Paragraphs for Which You Are Given the Information

For this exercise, you will be given all the information you need to write paragraphs recommending that field-service technicians get cellular phones for their vans.

CELLULAR PHONES FOR FIELD-SERVICE TECHNICIANS

Scott Goodyear is a field service technician for a digital equipment corporation. On Friday Scott had a terrible day. Scott travels in his van throughout New Brunswick servicing his customers' digital equipment. While on the road he periodically has to call into his office in Saint John to find out where he should go next. Then, he has to call the customer to get additional information and to tell the customer he is on his way.

Well, on that terrible Friday, Scott spent thirty minutes looking for a phone booth. He finally found a pay phone on the Trans-Canada in the middle of nowhere. He got the name of his next customer, but when he called her, the noise of the pick-ups and logging trucks speeding along the Trans-Canada was so loud that he could hardly hear a word she said.

He was sure the customer felt the company wasn't providing very good service, since it had taken him so long to call her. He also realized that the call hadn't done much for his company's image. "It's hard to sound professional while talking from a phone booth," Scott thought to himself. Scott was glad it hadn't been pouring rain or snowing!

Scott also felt he had wasted a lot of time that day. He could have made some more service calls if he had been able to get in touch with his company and his customers more quickly.

That Friday Scott decided to do something to solve the problem. That's why, on Monday morning, he is sitting down trying to write a memo to his supervisor recommending that field-service technicians get cellular phones for their vans. He knows his supervisor doesn't want to hear him whine about his bad day. Instead, in one or more paragraphs, Scott has to explain how providing cellular phones for the field technicians will be better for business.

Write the paragraphs for Scott.

Exercise 11: Writing Paragraphs for Which You Provide the Information

For this exercise, you will have to find the information you need. You may find this information by asking friends or instructors or by looking it up in the library or on the Internet. This exercise has two parts.

PROTECTING THE OFFICE NOTEBOOK COMPUTER

Your office has bought a notebook computer that any employee may sign out and take home. You read an article aloud to your supervisor warning people to protect their home computers from damage caused by electrical disturbances. You want to suggest to employees that before they use the office computer at home they buy a surge suppressor. Knowing you are trained at a technical college and thus are computer literate, your supervisor asks you to write a memo to all office staff.

He also suggests you explain what a surge suppressor is, why one is needed, where to get one, and how much one costs. "Make sure they don't confuse a surge suppressor with a power bar," your supervisor adds. Use the following format for your memo:

TO: All Staff

FROM: _____, Technologist

DATE: April 3, 199—

SUBJECT: Request for Staff to Use a Surge Suppressor with the Office Notebook

---

End your memo with your initials or your signature in the bottom left-hand corner.

PROTECTING YOURSELF WHILE USING THE OFFICE NOTEBOOK COMPUTER

Your memo on surge suppressors led to staff's asking you all kinds of questions about computers in the home. You decide to prepare an information sheet. You want to include a few paragraphs on "How to Set Up Your Computer Work Station Ergonomically." You want to include such details as what kind of lighting and what kind of chair to use. You'll also want to define "ergonomically." Write these few paragraphs for the information sheet.

Exercise 12: Writing Paragraphs for Which You Provide the Information

For this exercise, you will have to find the information you need. You may find this information by asking friends or instructors or by looking it up in the library or on the Internet.

OPENING A "SATELLITE" OFFICE

You work in the electrical training department of a large telecommunications firm in Kanata, Ontario.

Part of your job is to ensure that electricians are kept informed of what's going on in the telecommunications industry and within the company. To ensure employees are kept up-to-date, you organize training sessions and prepare a monthly newsletter that is distributed to all staff.

Company staff are asked to forward suggestions for topics they would like you to cover in the newsletter. Recently, several staff members have asked about the possibility of the company's setting up a "satellite office." Many of the staff members drive 50 to 60 kilometres to get to work and are getting weary of waiting in long traffic jams.

You know that in Ontario the telephone company has recently set up a satellite office 45 kilometres outside Ottawa in Renfrew, ON; fifteen of the company's employees who previously commuted from Renfrew to various telephone company offices now do their same jobs from the new satellite office located just minutes from their homes. Employees in the satellite office are linked to other offices via computer. These employees are "telecommuting."

You decide to write a few paragraphs comparing the advantages and disadvantages of satellite offices over conventional offices, where employees commute to one central location. Here are some points of comparison you may wish to include:

- social problems associated with commuting (e.g., traffic jams, pollution, parking, high costs of providing public transit)
- effects on employees (e.g., increased stress, lowered productivity).

Note: You will have to find the information you need for this paragraph. You may find this information by asking friends or instructors or by looking it up in the library or on the Internet. You may also use your own experience.

SOME BACKGROUND INFORMATION ON "TELECOMMUTING"

Instead of going to work at a central office, employees can use computers at home or at some other location to work on projects. The home computer is linked, via a telephone line, with a computer network or mainframe computer at a central office. These employees are said to be "telecommuting" to work.

Combining a computer with a communications link for two-way communication with other computers is called telecommunications. Two or more computers linked together via telephone lines form a computer network.

Telecommuting can succeed when the work can be done on a keyboard or by speaking over the telephone; it is not so well suited to personal service, inventory and storage, or physical work such as manufacturing.

Exercise 13: Writing Paragraphs in a Letter

THE THANK-YOU LETTER

Every year students are awarded bursaries to continue their studies. The foundations and companies awarding these bursaries expect to receive thank-you letters. The foundations and companies have asked students to include brief biographies and descriptions of career goals in their thank-you letters.

Below is a list of fictional bursaries available to students in different technologies. This list is taken from a *Student Financial Aid and Awards* booklet. Select one of the bursaries from the list and pretend that you have received it.

Write a thank-you letter. In your first paragraph thank the foundation or company for the bursary. In your last paragraph thank the foundation or company again. In your middle paragraphs include a brief biography and a description of your career goals. You should also include specific details of how you're going to use the bursary, so the foundation or company will know its money will be well spent.

Background Information on Bursaries (taken from a fictional Student Financial Aid and Awards booklet)

Bursaries are non-repayable awards ranging from $100 to $1,000. They are made possible through contributions from private companies, organizations, and individuals to the college's Scholarship and Bursary Fund.

To be considered for a bursary, a student must demonstrate financial need and have satisfactory academic standing. In some cases consideration is also given to the student's contribution to the college and/or the community. A student cannot apply for a bursary until successfully completing one term at the college.

List of Bursaries

The awards booklet lists 114 bursaries; we've listed only a few of those.

—**Alumni Bursaries**: an endowment established by the Alumni Association for students in business, engineering, and health.

—**Dr. Frances Brown and Mr. Tom Brown Fund**: a $200 bursary for a student in the School of Business.

—**High Tide Stevedoring Company Ltd.**: a $300 bursary available to a student in any technology, trade, or career program.

—**Jan Kovacs Memorial Bursary**: a $200 bursary in memory of Jan Kovacs, former Dean of the School of Business, for a student in the School of Business.

—**Orphans' Fund**: a bursary for students who are sole support parents or married students with dependents.

—**Parry Sound Dental Group**: a $300 bursary for a student in health.

—**Reynard Canada Inc**: a $500 bursary for a student in the School of Engineering or the School of Business.

—**Rodriques Family Fund**: an annual bursary for a student whose permanent residence is in Capreol, Chelmsford, Coniston, Copper Cliff, Espanola, or Sudbury.

—**Sine Wave Technologies Inc.**: a $250 bursary for a student in the electronics technology.

—**Tariq Khan Memorial Bursary**: an annual bursary for a student in any business, trades or technology program.

—**University Women's Club**: a $500 bursary for a student in any technology or trade.

—**Villeneuve Foundation**: an annual bursary for a student in Automotive Trades.

Complete this short exercise before you write your thank-you letter.

In the phrase "thank-you letter," "thank-you" is an adjective describing the noun "letter" ("thank-you" is called an adjective because it tells *what kind of* letter). The phrase "thank-you" has a hyphen when it is used as an adjective. In the expression "Thank you for your help," "thank you" is not an adjective and there is no hyphen. In the following sentences put in any hyphens that are needed:

1. Thank you for meeting with me to discuss employment with your company.

2. I hope you received my thank you note.

3. On behalf of all the students in my class, I would like to thank you for giving us a tour of your plant.

6

USING HEADINGS AND LISTS TO HELP YOUR READER

In all the chapters of this book, you have been learning how to look at your writing "through your reader's eyes" by considering your reader's needs and preferences. This final chapter takes "through your reader's eyes" literally: you will learn how to physically arrange your writing on the page in ways that make it easy for your reader to see how it is organized. You will learn to use headings and lists, so your reader can identify the major ideas immediately and locate details quickly and easily.

Using headings and lists also enables you to produce business and technical documents that create a favourable impression on your reader. Every time you communicate in school and in the workplace, you are doing two things: (1) getting the job done, and (2) making a statement about who you are and the kind of work you do. The skills you will acquire in this chapter will enable you to complete your writing tasks successfully and impress your reader as a professional.

Communication Outcomes

When you complete this chapter, you will be able to

- use headings to highlight each new topic in a letter, memo, or report
- explain the difference between **generic headings** and **content headings**
- explain the difference between headings and subheadings
- use subheadings to highlight subtopics in a letter, memo, or report
- explain why listing is used in technical and business writing
- use listing in your letters, memos, and reports, where appropriate.

Language Outcomes

When you have finished this chapter, you will be able to

- write headings and subheadings that are descriptive and concise
- use parallel structure when you write lists, headings, and subheadings
- use one of the following three styles when you write a list: complete sentences, partial sentences, or fragments
- write a lead-in sentence to introduce a stacked list.

HEADINGS

Why use headings?
Effective headings can

- help readers identify the main ideas of a document
- help readers pick out particular sections that interest them
- make a document attractive.

The following is a report on a chemical spill in a machine shop. Immediately following is the same report printed with headings. Look at the two reports to see how much easier it is to read the report with headings than the one without.

Note: An "incident report" describes an event in the workplace that either resulted in, or was likely to result in, injuries, damage to equipment, or lost production time. An incident report tells the reader what happened, what the consequences were, and what can be done to bring the workplace back to normal and to prevent such an event from happening again.

TO: Mohamed Taher, Safety Committee Chairperson

FROM: Francis Yee, Machine Shop Supervisor

DATE: 2 April 199—

SUBJECT: Chemical Spill in Machine Shop
(1 April 199—)

A 205-litre drum of hydraulic oil was spilled in the machine shop on Monday, April 1, at 2:30 p.m. No one was seriously hurt and the spill was contained and cleaned up, but we lost an hour's production.

The hydraulic oil for the hydraulic systems powering our equipment is stored in drums in the warehouse. On Monday afternoon Cliff Panchyson, the shift supervisor, phoned the warehouse for two drums. A new warehouse worker, Bill Low, brought the drums in with the big diesel forklift instead of with the electric pallet-carrier they normally use. I was in my office.

At 2:30 p.m. I heard a crash and some shouting, so I went into the machine shop. I saw the forklift stuck against Lathe #2, both drums on the floor, one drum split open and pouring hydraulic oil everywhere. Two shop workers had slipped and fallen, probably because the oil had made the floor slippery.

I switched off the power to the equipment, and Cliff Panchyson chased all the workers outside. I sent the two workers who had fallen (Gale Adams and Hans van Weerden) to the first aid station. The first aid attendant said they were fine but sent them home for the day. I erected dams around the spill to prevent any oil from getting into the sewer system. Cliff and I then put an absorbent clay on the oil to prevent it from spreading. Cliff swept up the clay, which had absorbed the oil, scooped it into a wheelbarrow, and transferred it into a drum. At 3:30 p.m. the safety officer, Theng Ong, determined that the spill had been contained and then cleaned up. The shop resumed production at 3:45 p.m.

I think we should overhaul Lathe #2, order an extra drum of hydraulic oil, and call for a safety committee meeting to make recommendations for the safe transporting of these drums.

Francis Yee

TO: Mohamed Taher, Safety Committee Chairperson
FROM: Francis Yee, Machine Shop Supervisor
DATE: 2 April 199—
SUBJECT: Chemical Spill in Machine Shop (April 1, 199—)

SUMMARY

A 205-litre drum of hydraulic oil was spilled in the machine shop on Monday, April 1, at 2:30 pm. No one was seriously hurt and the spill was contained and cleaned up, but we lost an hour's production.

BACKGROUND

The hydraulic oil for the hydraulic systems powering our equipment is stored in drums in the warehouse. On Monday afternoon Cliff Panchyson, the shift supervisor, phoned the warehouse for two drums. A new warehouse worker, Bill Low, brought the drums in with the big diesel forklift instead of with the electric pallet-carrier they normally use. I was in my office.

INCIDENT

At 2:30 p.m. I heard a crash and some shouting, so I went into the machine shop. I saw the forklift stuck against Lathe #2, both drums on the floor, one drum split open and pouring hydraulic oil everywhere. Two shop workers had slipped and fallen, probably because the oil had made the floor slippery.

ACTION TAKEN

I switched off the power to the equipment, and Cliff Panchyson chased all the workers outside. I sent the two workers who had fallen (Gale Adams and Hans van Weerden) to the first aid station. The first aid attendant said they were fine but sent them home for the day. I erected dams around the spill to prevent any oil from getting into the sewer system. Cliff and I then put an absorbent clay on the oil to prevent it from spreading. Cliff swept up the clay, which had absorbed the oil; scooped it into a wheelbarrow; and transferred it into a drum. At 3:30 p.m. the safety officer, Theng Ong, determined that the spill had been contained and then cleaned up. The shop resumed production at 3:45 p.m.

RECOMMENDATIONS

I think we should overhaul Lathe #2, order an extra drum of hydraulic oil, and call for a safety committee meeting to make recommendations for the safe transporting of these drums.

Francis Yee

GUIDELINE 26:

Use headings to highlight each *new topic* in a long letter, memo, or report. You can make a heading for a page, a section, or a paragraph.

The incident report you have just read is in standard memo format. The report has five paragraphs. Each paragraph has a special function, and the heading allows the reader to identify that function immediately. The headings also allow the readers to refer easily to all sections of the report; for example, if I asked you what the recommendations in the report were, you would be able to answer my question quickly *if you had the report with headings.*

The headings in this incident report are called *generic headings*. The word "generic" means "referring to a kind, class, or group." The incident report headings are called "generic" because the headings tell the reader *what kind of* information to expect and would be the same for all incident reports regardless of the content of the individual report. Thus, every incident report could have each of the following headings: summary, background, incident, action taken, and recommendations. The company might even have an incident report form with these headings preprinted, so the worker writing out the report would only have to fill in the details under each heading. Whenever the headings are so general that they would remain the same regardless of the particular details, the headings are called generic.

There is one other kind of heading, called the *content heading*. Content headings name the particular details (the content) and thus change according to what the details are. You may use generic headings and content headings in the same report.

KEY TERMS

GENERIC AND CONTENT HEADINGS: Generic headings tell the reader what kind of information to expect. An example of a generic heading is "Introduction."

Content headings name a group of details for the reader, so the reader will know what further details to expect. An example of a content heading is "Cost of Car Alarms."

You can learn which generic headings to use in which reports by taking a communication course, reading a communication textbook, or looking at model reports. You can write your own content headings by naming each group of details.

HEADINGS AND SUBHEADINGS

Here is an example of the recommendations section of an incident report that uses both a generic heading and two content headings.

RECOMMENDATIONS

Training of Maintenance Personnel

1. Train all current maintenance personnel on the machinery and equipment used in the sawmill.
2. When a maintenance worker leaves and a replacement is hired, train the replacement.
3. Use outside instructors who can devote uninterrupted time to training.

Daily Downtime Chart

4. Instruct the head millwright to keep a daily downtime chart showing
— the time of day the stoppage occurred
— the length of time the stoppage lasted
— the machine or equipment
— a short description of what happened
— the total time lost that day.

Notice how the two content headings, Training of Maintenance Personnel and Daily Downtime Chart, are specific to that particular incident report and could not be used in the incident report you read earlier on the spill in the machine shop.

Notice also that RECOMMENDATIONS is in all capital letters, whereas Training of Maintenance Personnel and Daily Downtime Chart only have the first letters of the main words capitalized. This is because Maintenance Personnel and Daily Downtime Chart are **subheadings under** the heading Recommendations.

GUIDELINE 27:

Use headings to highlight topics; use subheadings to highlight subtopics. Make sure your reader can tell your headings from your subheadings. Make sure your reader can tell which subheadings go with which heading. You can do this either by

- using all capital letters for your headings and lower case letters for your subheadings
  OR
- indenting subheadings so they are farther from the left margin than your headings
  OR
- using the "engineering numbering system," in which the first heading would be numbered *1*, the first subheading under heading *1* would be numbered *1.1*, etc.).

Practice

Complete this simple exercise on the difference between headings and subheadings.

The following is from a typical department store directory you would see at the main escalator or in the elevator. The only difference is that we've jumbled the directory so you can't tell the departments from the sections within departments. Your task is to rewrite the directory so the reader can tell the difference between departments (headings) and sections (subheadings).

furniture	dresses	slacks	women's clothing
hats	suits	stationery	men's clothing
gloves	dining room sets	dress shirts	pens
envelopes	accessories	lamps	writing desks

Here is a page from a comparison report. While you read it, notice how the writer has used headings, subheadings, and the engineering numbering system to show the reader how each section is related to every other section.

---

1. PERFORMANCE

Performance is the most important criterion in selecting a truck for our warehouse because of the large travel areas and the continuous shifts worked.

1.1 Power: Three trucks of the seven tested met the required horsepower ratings. Of these three, the Spearing was the most powerful and thus would be the least stressed. The Kraftgabel ranked second in power output, and the Martin ranked third.

1.2 Lift capacity: Two trucks successfully completed our loading test: the Spearing and the Kraftgabel. The Spearing can lift 2 000 kg to 3.275 m in 7.8 s. The Kraftgabel can lift 2 500 kg to 3.275 m in 10.9 s.

1.3 Speed: The fastest truck we tested was the Martin. Our test simulated the conditions in the warehouse and the yard. Absolute top speed is not practical in our work, but the figures in Appendix 3 indicate that the Martin would be less stressed in to-and-fro travel than the other trucks.

2. MANOEUVRABILITY

The selected truck should be able to operate in confined spaces such as railcars, truck beds, and pallet-storage aisles in the warehouse.

2.1 Turning radius: All trucks tested could turn around within the prescribed widths.

2.2 Lift height: The Kraftgabel has by far the greatest maximum lift height: 4.5 m. This reach would enable us to double the existing storage capacity while using the same floor area.

2.3 Tires: Most manufacturers advise that the solid "cushion" tires are not suitable for extended outdoor use. We therefore tested four trucks that are offered with a choice of either cushion <u>or</u> pneumatic tires....

(and so on)

Note: In this case the reader easily sees that the writer's ideas are organized in a particular way. If the paragraphs and subparagraphs were not clearly distinguished, a reader would not see the *relationship* between the sections.

So far we have been looking at headings and subheadings in reports, one of which was in memo format. Letters also have headings. Read the following letter and pay particular attention to the headings and subheadings. How does the writer distinguish headings from subheadings?

Chapman, Charlesworth and Chiu Advertising

108 Raven Crescent
Prince Rupert, BC V8J 1B9

November 6, 199—
Ms. Lili Volek
President
Clean Water, Inc.
2210 Seal Cove Circle
Prince Rupert, BC V8J 1B9

Dear Ms. Volek

SUBJECT: PERSONALIZED LICENCE PLATES TO ADVERTISE YOUR COMPANY

I am still enthusiastic about your idea of a personalized licence plate as another way to advertise your business. Here is the information you requested on the application procedure, the regulations, and the cost. I have also included some suggestions for you of advertising slogans for the plates.

APPLICATION PROCEDURE

BC's personalized licence plate program has been administered by the Insurance Corporation of British Columbia (ICBC) since August 1991. You can pick up an application form at any Autoplan agency. You have to bring proof of vehicle ownership (your registration papers) and up to five slogan selections. You return the completed form to the Autoplan agency. Expect to wait about sixty days for your application to be processed.

When two or more people want the same slogan, the rule is "First come, first served." Of course, you cannot have a slogan that is already taken.

REGULATIONS

I have summarized the regulations for you below. You can obtain a complete copy of the regulations from any Autoplan agency.

Type of Vehicle: You can not use personalized licence plates on motorcycles, trailers, trucks, vans over 3 700 kilograms, or antique cars with vintage plates. You may use them on all other vehicles.

SLOGAN

Type of Characters: You can use Roman letters and Arabic numerals. While you can use all letters, you can not use all numerals. Any other symbols, such as #, * or @, are forbidden because they are too difficult to identify and don't fit ICBC computer programs.

Ms. Lili Volek
November 6, 199—
Page 2

Number of Characters: The maximum number of characters is six. The minimum is two. You can insert a blank space or a hyphen to separate the text at any point as, for example, in "I X CEL."

Unacceptable Slogans:

- You can not use character combinations that could make it difficult for people, such as the police, to identify you. Thus, you could not use "8B2Z38" because an "8" and a "B" or a "3" and an "8" are easily confused. Similarly, a "2" and a "Z" could be confused.
- You also can not use the prefixes BC and MD.
- You can not use slogans that promote substance abuse or unsafe driving. Thus, you couldn't use "HIT ME."
- You can not use anything that is offensive, suggestive, or not in good taste. For example, "ORPXES" was not allowed because of the message when you read it backwards.

COST

Personalized plates cost $50 a set plus $24 a year for the renewal fee. Replacements are $15.

SUGGESTIONS FOR SLOGANS

Here are my suggestions in order of preference. They are all self-explanatory except where I've included an explanation.

CLN H2O
1DR H2O
H2O 14U (Water one for you—a play on "Order one for you")
PRO H2O
CLR H2O
H2O PRO

If you have any questions or want to discuss the idea further, please call me at 434-5734. I think it's a great idea and look forward to seeing your new plates.

Sincerely

Eric Chiu

Eric Chiu
Director

PARALLELISM IN HEADINGS AND SUBHEADINGS

Look at these headings:

Bad Sample

1. TRUCK REPAIRS
2. CARS
3. TRACTOR INFORMATION
4. WORKING ON BULLDOZERS

The different wordings of the four headings suggests that the information is poorly organized; for example, the headings suggest that while the first section is about truck repairs, the second section includes much more information about cars than just repairs.

Better Sample

1. REPAIRING TRUCKS
2. REPAIRING CARS
3. REPAIRING TRACTORS
4. REPAIRING BULLDOZERS

This is better but boring.

Good Samples

1.   VEHICLE REPAIRS
1.1 Trucks
1.2 Cars
1.3 Tractors
1.4 Bulldozers

or if the report contains *no other topic*:

VEHICLE REPAIRS
1. Trucks
2. Cars
3. Tractors
4. Bulldozers

GUIDELINE 28:

Make headings or subheadings alike, or parallel, in their wording.

Practice

Arrange this list of report headings into headings, subheadings, and sub-subheadings, so the reader can easily distinguish the different levels of headings. You may rewrite any of these headings. Make sure your headings are parallel.

WELDCO LTD	CHARGE HAND	EXPLOSIVE WELDING DONE AT SHERBROOKE	CLOSING DOWN JOLIETTE SHOP
PERSONNEL	THE LABOURERS		CLOSING THE SOREL SHOP
CHIEF ENGINEER	DRIVING STAFF	EXPLOSIVE WELDING CARRIED OUT IN MONTREAL	NEW BRANCHES
THE CHIEF ENGINEER'S ASSISTANT	MANUFACTURING PROCESSES		DRUMMONDVILLE
C.E.'S RESEARCH ASSISTANT	WELDING		TROIS RIVIERES
PRODUCTION MANAGER	ARC WELDING	FUTURE PLANS	
SUPERVISOR	GAS WELDING	BRANCHES TO BE CLOSED DOWN	
	EXPLOSIVE WELDING		

In case you're curious about welding, here are some details: In *arc welding* an electric arc between an electrode and the workpiece is used to heat the metal to be joined. In *gas welding* the metals are melted together with a flame from a torch that is burning oxygen and some other combustible gas. In *explosive welding* the metals are forced together by detonating an explosive.

LISTS

Why use lists?

Lists help your reader find information quickly and easily. You can use lists in all your workplace documents, from e-mail messages to letters to formal reports.

You can make a list from single words or from whole sentences. The effect of good listing is

- *to concentrate* a number of important points

- *to arrange* them in a clear sequence

- *to break up* the monotony of a mass of written text

- to make information *quickly available* to readers.

You have just read a list. If you wrote out that information in consecutive or combined sentences, your text would be dense and difficult to read.

The list you have read is called a **stacked** list because **the items in the list are placed or stacked one on top of the other.**

Writing a Parallel List

Earlier in this chapter, you learned about the importance of making your headings and subheadings alike in their wording (parallel). You also need to use parallelism when you write a list, whether the items in your list are part of a sentence or part of a stacked list.

To be parallel, all items in a list must use the same grammatical form. Each item in a list should also fit with the introduction to the list. A list with these qualities is "parallel."

Here is an example of a sentence with parallel ideas:

Landscape and horticultural technicians and specialists survey and assess landscapes, draw sketches and build models of landscape designs, and construct and maintain gardens, parks, golf courses, and other landscaped environments.

This sentence uses simple present tense verbs to describe what landscape and horticultural technicians do, e.g., survey, assess, draw, build, construct, maintain.

The ideas in the following sentences are *not* parallel.

We need accountants who know how to communicate in an effective way, are logical thinkers, and who have the ability to analyze situations carefully.

Because the ideas are not alike in their wording, the sentence sounds awkward and confusing. One way to make the ideas parallel would be to rewrite the sentence, so that each item in the list completed the phrase "accountants who know how to" and thus began with a verb:

We need accountants who know how to communicate effectively, think logically, and analyze situations carefully.

 GUIDELINE 29:

When you use a stacked list or a list as part of a sentence, make the items in the list alike, or parallel, in their wording.

Here is a parallel stacked list:

All company drivers should

- lock their trucks at 4 p.m.
- leave the truck key with security
- sign truck keys in and out.

You can see that each part begins with an active verb. Since each part continues the introductory sentence, no part needs a capital letter, although capital letters are sometimes used for emphasis.

The following list is *not* parallel.

Work completed by February 23:

1. We finished the foundation.
2. Drains sealed.
3. Painting the door frames.
4. Surfaced driveway.

Can you see why the list is not parallel? The first item is a complete sentence with a subject and a verb. The other three items are not complete sentences. The second item is a fragment using the passive voice—[The] drains [were] sealed. The third item uses the gerund (the -ing form of the verb). The fourth item is a fragment, but in the active voice—[We] surfaced [the] driveway.

Because none of the items match, the list you just read above looks like a jumble of random notes. It makes the information harder for the reader to understand.

The following list *is* parallel and easier to read.

Work completed by February 23:

1. Foundation finished
2. Drains sealed
3. Door frames painted
4. Driveway surfaced.

Can you see why the list is now parallel?

Introducing a List

Introduce a stacked list with a **lead-in**. The lead-in can be a word, a partial sentence or a complete sentence. Here are three examples of ways to introduce stacked lists:

Staff:

— Mill Superintendent
— Shift Supervisors
— Operators

I recommend that we

— open at 7 a.m.
— employ an extra person at the front desk
— double our security during lunch hours.

Your career planning strategy should include three steps:

1. Do a self-assessment of your own interests, values, aptitudes, and transferrable skills to help identify the kinds of work you will find most rewarding.

2. Use labour market information to ensure your career-planning decisions are in line with labour market demand.

3. Prepare an action plan, using the information you gathered in steps 1 and 2.

Use a colon (:) to punctuate your lead-in when the lead-in is a complete sentence, as in the third example above. You may also use a colon when you have a one-word lead-in, since the colon means the same as an equal sign.

GUIDELINE 30:

Use a word, fragment, or sentence to introduce a stacked list.

Choosing the Appearance of a List

Indent lists so that they stand out strongly in the text. If possible provide white space equally on both sides of the list. Look back at the three lists above to see the effects of white space.

Use symbols to itemize the parts of a list:

- This list uses bullets.

- Sequences of instructions always use numbers as symbols.

- Letter symbols are less clear and less emphatic than bullets or numbers.

- Some writers use dashes—like this.

- You may use other symbols, but make sure they are appropriate; for example, check-marks should only be used for items that can be checked off or ticked as having been completed. Such symbols as hearts or bombs are rarely appropriate.

Choosing the Style of a List

When writing a list you can choose one of three styles:

1. Complete sentences
2. Partial sentences
3. Fragments.

The list you've just read is made up of fragments. The section you read about Introducing a List illustrates all three styles of lists: the first list in the section is made up of fragments, the second list is made up of partial sentences, and the third list is made up of complete sentences. You may choose whichever style you like to make the list effective.

The paragraph you just read contains information that would be even clearer in the form of a list, but by this stage you are probably happy to see some unbroken text!

Each item in a list made up of complete sentences may consist of more than one sentence. Here is an example of a list where each item is a short paragraph called a subparagraph.

FOUR DEVICES FOR THEFT-PROOFING YOUR CAR

Here is a brief description of four devices on the market for theft-proofing your car, along with their prices:

1. *Car Alarms*. $100 to $1,000. The alarms are activated by noise or shock sensors. Purchase an alarm that is loud enough to scare off a thief.
2. *Steering-Wheel Locks*. $35 to $70. The most common one looks like a stick with an umbrella handle at each end. It locks the steering-wheel and the brake pedal so the car can't be steered or braked. Some models lock only the steering-wheel.
3. *Ignition Disablers*. $20. A hidden toggle switch grounds out the distributor so the car can't be started.
4. *Decals*. $2. This decal says your car is protected by a surveillance company.

Practice

Change this list so that it is parallel.

RULES FOR USING DEBIT CARDS

When using debit cards, consumers should follow the rules below, which are the same as those for using credit cards and managing money wisely.

- Don't let anyone else use your bank card. Don't give anyone else your PIN.
- Just because it's convenient is not a good reason for buying an item with your debit card.
- The question to ask yourself is whether you'd still buy the item if you had to pay cash. The important question is whether the item is within your budget.
- Debit card purchases must be recorded in your chequebook immediately. Bank statements should be checked promptly to make sure your debit card purchases have been recorded correctly. Report any mistakes to the bank immediately.

Rewrite the memo on the next page to make it easier to read by including a list.

Fill in the "To," "From," "Date," and "Subject."

TO:

FROM:

DATE:

SUBJECT:

Please repair the heating and cooling system in SW3-3795.

It was decided that the two radiators on the east side would be controlled by the room thermostat; and further, that the air handling unit on the roof be serviced so that no unwanted cold air infiltrated the room.

The heating and cooling thermostats should be set up so that they don't "fight" each other.

If you have any questions, please call me at Local 7185.

REVIEW QUESTIONS

In your own words, answer the following questions.

1. Name three functions of headings.

   _____

   _____

   _____

   _____

2. How can you make sure your reader can tell which subheadings go with which headings?

   _____

   _____

   _____

   _____

3. What does parallel mean?

   _____

   _____

4. What are the four symbols you can use to itemize the parts of a list?

   _____

   _____

5. What are the three styles you can use when writing a list?

   _____

   _____

QUESTION SHEET

List any questions you have about this chapter.

Questions

_____

_____

_____

_____

_____

_____

_____

_____

_____

_____

Answers

_____

_____

_____

_____

_____

_____

_____

_____

_____

_____

_____

EXERCISES

Exercise 1: Writing Parallel Lists

This exercise has three parts. In Part 1, you will have to revise some sentences to correct errors in parallel structure. In Part 2, you will have to put information from sentences into a stacked list. In Part 3, you will have to put information from stacked lists into complete sentences.

Part 1

Revise these sentences to improve parallel structure.

Systems Analysis and Design

1. Systems analysis and design is a seven-step process used to solve problems in a company's computer system by developing a new computer system or to make modifications to an old system.

   _____

   _____

   _____

2. A systems analyst, the key person in the systems analysis and design process, acts as a go-between for the people who use the system and information professionals.

   _____

   _____

   _____

3. In the systems analysis and design process, the analyst first defines the process and a feasibility study is done.

   _____

   _____

   _____

Uses of Personal Computers

4. Most people's computer needs fall into one of three broad categories: personal, doing work for school, or work-related.

   _____

   _____

   _____

5. Personal uses of the computer include home budgeting, corresponding, telecommunications, and doing volunteer activities.

   _____

   _____

   _____

6. School-related computer uses include papers, doing research with electronic data bases, computer programs are sometimes written, and using computer software to complete homework projects.

_____

_____

_____

7. Some people use personal computers for managing small businesses or to do work that they brought home from the office.

_____

_____

_____

Part 2

Put the information from the specified sentences into a stacked list.

1. Write a stacked list using the information from Part 1, sentence 4. Remember to use a lead-in sentence and keep the items in your list parallel.

_____

_____

_____

2. Write a stacked list using the information from Part 1, sentence 6. Remember to use a lead-in sentence and keep the items in your list parallel.

_____

_____

_____

3. Put the information from the following sentences into a stacked list. First, you'll have to revise the second sentence to correct errors in parallel structure.

_____

_____

_____

HOW TO SELECT COMPUTER SOFTWARE

You can select software in several ways. You can read articles about software, sometimes members of a user's group can give you information, a salesperson at a computer store can help you if you explain your needs, or use the software at work or school.

4. Put the information from the following sentences into a stacked parallel list. First, you will have to revise the sentences to correct errors in parallel structure:

MAIN DUTIES OF COMPUTER PROGRAMMERS
Computer programmers write computer programs or software packages. They test, debug, document, and implement computer programs or software packages. As well, when required, minor modifications are made to maintain existing computer programs. Computer programmers may also be involved in solving computer problems for computer users. Helping to develop and customize company software applications is another area of responsibility.

Part 3

Write a sentence using the information from each of the following stacked lists.

1. Wide Area Networks

Wide area networks (WANs) are used for computer communications over long distances. The three types of WANs include

- value-added networks
- private networks
- specialized networks.

---

2. Uses of Telecommunications

Telecommunications is used to

- find information
- interact with others
- send and receive electronic mail
- work from home using a computer.

---

3. Responsibilities of Computer Systems Analysts

Computer systems analysts are responsible for

- analyzing information-processing or computation needs
- designing computer systems that meet these needs or performing the necessary computations
- analyzing data bases
- supervising computer programmers.

_____

_____

_____

_____

Exercise 2: Rewriting Paragraphs to Add Headings and Lists

Students sometimes have this complaint: They receive one practice writing assignment that they complete and go over with their teacher, and then they receive a second assignment— often one that is graded—that is very different from the first practice assignment. That complaint makes some sense. Therefore, this exercise consists of two assignments that are very similar to each other. Write the first practice and go over it with your teacher. Then, see how much easier it is for you to write the second assignment!

Part 1: Information on BC Ferries' Regulations for Passengers

Read the following paragraph. The paragraph is written to explain BC Ferries' regulations to its passengers.

BC Ferries enforces regulations for public health and safety. BC Ferries also enforces regulations to enable cars and passengers to board the ferries quickly, so the ferries can depart on time. Smoking is allowed only on outside passenger decks. A car may not carry more than one 25-litre container of gasoline, empty or full. Not more than two portable 25-litre containers of gasoline, empty or full, can be carried on a motorboat or recreational vehicle. Tickets can be purchased with cash, travellers cheques, or VISA and MasterCard. A recreational vehicle can carry no more than two cylinders of propane. Cylinders of propane must be safely secured to the vehicle in an upright position. You have to close and tag the valves on all cylinders of propane. Walk-on passengers must purchase tickets at least ten minutes before the scheduled sailing; drivers must purchase tickets for vehicles at least five minutes before sailing. We will refuse to allow anyone on board who is apparently under the influence of drugs or alcohol. No vehicles that appear to be in unsafe condition will be allowed on board.

Rewrite the paragraph for BC Ferries' passengers. Use a major heading for the entire paragraph and use subheadings. Use stacked parallel lists with lead-ins.

Part 2: Information on BC Ferries' Fares

Read the paragraph below, which explains BC Ferries' fares to tourists to BC.

For the average tourist taking the BC Ferries from Horseshoe Bay to Langdale there are three different fares. The fare for a walk-on passenger is $6.75 return during the shoulder season (March 24 to June 25; September 8 to November 16; December 18 to June 4), and $7 during the low (November 17 to December 17) and the peak (June 26 to September 7) seasons. For a driver with a car, the cost is $25.75 round trip for the car during the peak, $23.25 during the shoulder, and $20.75 during the low seasons. The fare for the driver and for each car passenger is the same as that for a walk-on passenger. For a walk-on passenger with a bicycle, kayak, or canoe, the round-trip fare, in addition to the $7 or $6.75 walk-on passenger fare, is $2.50 for the bicycle, $4 for the kayak, and $4 for the canoe. Walk-on passengers can purchase tickets at the walk-in entrance at the ferry terminal. For drivers to purchase tickets, there is a drive-through entrance. BC Seniors can travel free as car passengers or as walk-on passengers on Monday through Thursday, except when any of these days is a holiday. The fee for a child aged five to eleven is $3.50 as a car passenger or walk-on passenger. Children under five are free. BC Seniors must show their BC GoldCare Cards. For more information, visit BC Ferries' Internet web site at http://www.bcferries.bc.ca.

The paragraph you have just read contains important information for drivers and for walk-on passengers on the BC Ferries. Rewrite the paragraph so drivers and walk-on passengers can find the information relevant to *them* quickly and easily. Use a major heading for the entire paragraph and use subheadings. Use stacked parallel lists introduced by lead-ins.

Exercise 3: Organizing Information in a Memo

This exercise is your opportunity to review everything you have learned. The exercise consists of two memos for you to rewrite: the Volunteers Memo and the Memo on Reducing Vehicle Theft.

THE VOLUNTEERS MEMO

Rewrite this memo by

- putting the main idea first
- making the information more accessible to the reader
- ending with a precise action.

TO: All Staff
FROM: Janis Zeidaks, Personnel Director
DATE: January 1, 199—
SUBJECT: Request for Staff Input

Many of us at our company find that we often could use the help of translators when dealing with our clients and their families. Some staff have volunteered to serve as translators. As a result we have translators available in Afrikaans, Chinese, Croatian, Dutch, Fijian, French, German, Hungarian, Hindi, Italian, Korean, Norwegian, Polish, Punjabi, Spanish, Urdu, and Swahili. For Chinese, we have people who speak Cantonese and Mandarin. We also have someone who can translate Wet'suwet'en. Even though we have volunteers for the languages I've mentioned, if *you too* can translate those languages, we'd still like to hear from you because we want to compile a list of volunteers for each language and want to have more than one volunteer for each language.

For people who volunteer, we need to have your phone local and, of course, the language you can translate. Don't forget to include the dialect. We will keep your name on file in Personnel and then staff who need translators can call us to get your phone number. We want to have our list complete as soon as possible. We want to send out an announcement soon to all staff telling them which languages are available.

J. Z.

MEMO ON REDUCING VEHICLE THEFTS

You are on the board of a housing co-operative. Since you moved into the co-op two years ago, you've noticed a sharp increase in the number of thefts from vehicles parked in the co-op's underground parking lot.

The issue of how to prevent thefts came up again at the last member's meeting. You volunteer to post a memo on the bulletin board near the first-floor entrance listing some actions members can take to reduce the chances of someone's breaking into their vehicles.

You talk to the local RCMP to get some information on preventing break-ins. "Be sure to let people know that they should call us if they see suspicious persons around a vehicle," says the RCMP constable at the end of your telephone conversation. Here are your notes from the conversation:

> — don't forget to close the windows and check that all doors have been locked if you leave your vehicle unattended, even if you're only leaving your vehicle for a few minutes
>
> — it's a good idea to put any valuables in the trunk, instead of just leaving them in the car, and don't forget to lock the trunk
>
> — an auto alarm system could be installed
>
> — items such as car stereos and radar detectors are easy to remove, so these should be engraved with your driver's licence number
>
> — if you're worried about vandalism, you might want to install a locking gas cap
>
> — leaving your house keys or garage door opener in the car is not a good idea

Write the memo to all co-op members:

- Put the main idea first.
- Eliminate wordiness.
- Put the suggestions on how to reduce theft into a stacked parallel list.
- End with an action.

Exercise 4: Organizing Information in a Letter

LETTER TO STORE MANAGER

You've been working full-time at a drug store near your home to save up money to go to school. The store manager is very pleased with your work, feels you have a lot of talent, and is happy to see you furthering your education. The manager would like you to continue to work at the store during the school term. The manager asks you to write a letter stating how many hours you would like to work, explaining why you are no longer full-time (this is required for the company's personnel records), and giving your availability. Since the store is near your home and you live near your school, you are available most times when you don't have classes.

Write the letter to the store manager. Invent the details of your availability based on your own schedule of classes. Use full letter format. Make up the name of the store, the store manager, the address, and any other details you need.

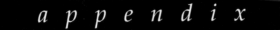

GUIDELINES

GUIDELINE 1 (p.5):
State your purpose at the beginning of your letters and memos.

GUIDELINE 2 (p.5):
Phrase your purpose statement by answering the question "What do I want my reader to do?"

GUIDELINE 3 (p.6):
Include *all* your probable readers when you write.

GUIDELINE 4 (p.8):
Prepare an outline before you write.

GUIDELINE 5 (p.11):
Put your main idea first and end with a precise action.

GUIDELINE 6 (p.17):
Use a standard Canadian format when writing your letters and memos.

GUIDELINE 7 (p.24):
Give your memos and letters subject lines that are both specific and concise. Be positive: Avoid negative subject lines.

GUIDELINE 8 (p.58):
In general, use *active* sentences for business and technical writing.

GUIDELINE 9 (p.61):
Show your reader what your sentence is about right away, in the first few words.

GUIDELINE 10 (p.63):
State your main idea directly, but take into account your relationship to your reader, your purpose, and your situation. Use a diplomatic supporting phrase or sentence when you feel the main idea alone would be too abrupt.

GUIDELINE 11 (p.79):
Combine sentences to show the relationship between your ideas and to add variety to your writing.

GUIDELINE 12 (p.98):
Read your writing aloud to make sure you are "talking" to your reader in a natural, straightforward style.

GUIDELINE 13 (p.99):
Use an English-English dictionary to make sure that the words you use are standard and appropriate to the context.

GUIDELINE 14 (p.99):
Use natural, everyday words with which your reader is familiar.

GUIDELINE 15 (p.100):
Do *not* use overused expressions or business jargon.

GUIDELINE 16 (p.101):
Do *not* use trendy expressions and slang.

GUIDELINE 17 (p.105):

Put you and your reader into your writing.

GUIDELINE 18 (p.107):

Eliminate unnecessary words in your writing.

GUIDELINE 19 (p.113):

Replace imprecise words with specific and measurable information whenever possible.

GUIDELINE 20 (p.130):

Limit the length of your paragraphs to a maximum of about seven typed lines.

GUIDELINE 21 (p.130):

Use white space so your reader can see quickly and easily where each paragraph ends and the next paragraph begins.

GUIDELINE 22 (p.130):

Begin each of your paragraphs with a main idea sentence that tells your reader what your paragraph is about. To complete your paragraph, add any supporting details needed to answer your reader's questions about the main idea.

GUIDELINE 23 (p.133):

Use supporting detail sentences in a paragraph to support the main idea of the paragraph in any one of five ways.

GUIDELINE 24 (p.134):

Use signposts and repetition of key words in your paragraphs to lead your reader from your main idea sentence to your supporting sentences, and from one supporting sentence to the next.

GUIDELINE 25 (p.135):

Plan each of your paragraphs by asking yourself

- What is the main idea of this paragraph? What do I want my reader to know? Turn your answer into a main idea sentence.
- What must I next tell my reader to support my main point? Answer all your reader's questions. Turn your answers into supporting detail sentences.

GUIDELINE 26 (p.169):

Use headings to highlight each new topic in a long letter, memo, or report. You can make a heading for a page, a section, or a paragraph.

GUIDELINE 27 (p.170):

Use headings to highlight topics; use subheadings to highlight subtopics. Make sure your reader can tell your headings from your subheadings. Make sure your reader can tell which subheadings go with which heading. You can do this either by

- using all capital letters for your headings and lowercase letters for your subheadings OR
- indenting subheadings so they are farther from the left margin than your headings OR
- using the "engineering numbering system," in which the first heading would be numbered *1*, the first subheading under heading *1* would be numbered *1.1*, etc.

GUIDELINE 28 (p.174):

Make headings or subheadings alike, or parallel, in their wording.

GUIDELINE 29 (p.176):

When you use a stacked list or a list as part of a sentence, make the items in the list alike, or parallel, in their wording.

GUIDELINE 30 (p.177):

Use a word, fragment, or sentence to introduce a stacked list.

Marquis Book Printing Inc.

Québec, Canada